THE NIC&TINE TRICK

THE TOTALLY NEW WAY TO STOP SMOKING

NEIL CASEY

metro

Published by Metro Publishing Ltd, 3 Bramber Court,
2 Bramber Road, London W14 9PB, England

British Library Cataloguing in Publication Data.
A CIPrecord of this book is available on request from
the British Library.

ISBN 1 84358 051 9

3 5 7 9 10 8 6 4 2

Design by ENVY

Printed and bound in Great Britain by BookMarque,
Croydon, Surrey

Papers used by Metro Publishing Ltd are natural,
recyclable products made from wood grown in sustainable forests.
The manufacturing processes conform to the environmental
regulations of the country of origin.

DISCLAIMER
In researching the nicotine trick, I have used information from the following sources:

UK government white paper, *Smoking Kills*
US Surgeon General
The Royal College Of Surgeons
The World Health Organization
Tobacco Industry declassified documents

Despite my extensive use of scientific information from these sources, I wish to
acknowledge that the conclusions reached in this book are mine, and I make no
attempt to ascribe my own views or conclusions to any of these organisations.

Contents

PART THREE – ANTI-CLIMAX

Introduction

The two biggest human obsessions are pleasure and death. Usually, the search for pleasure and the fear of death never come into conflict. But when they do, the result is an obsessive craving that can destroy everything in its path.

On the surface of it, the precise reason for smoking a cigarette is a mystery, even to most smokers.

ON THE SURFACE of it, the precise reason for smoking a cigarette is a mystery, even to most smokers.

Everyone knows that smoking causes lung cancer, heart disease, impotence and high blood pressure, yet smokers repeatedly choose to take this risk, even though they can't explain why. The urge for survival is built into every human being on the planet, yet more than a billion people are going directly against this instinct. Why? Surely there's no instinct stronger than the fear of death.

Actually, there is…

… *but only one.*

My name is Neil Casey. For two decades, my affair with cigarettes tormented me day and night. I've smoked through severe bouts of flu. I've smoked in an aircraft toilet. I've smoked inside hospitals. I once smoked a cigarette I retrieved from the floor of a motorway service station toilet (after drying it against my car heater). I've begged, borrowed and, on one occasion, even stolen a cigarette.

I've smoked with food, I've smoked with beer, wine, whisky, vodka, coffee, tea, orange juice, water. I've smoked in rain, snow and bright sunshine. I've rolled thousands of cigarettes. I've bought hundreds of lighters. I've offended countless non-smokers. I've smoked half-finished cigarettes from ashtrays. I've inhaled cigars. I've crawled around the floor of my flat looking for just enough stale tobacco to roll one more cigarette. I've taken filters off cigarettes just so I could get more of a 'hit'. I once risked death trying to retrieve a packet of cigarettes that I dropped off a fairground ride. I've smoked until I could smell the tobacco on my own face.

I've humiliated, embarrassed and demeaned myself, all in the name of smoking just one more cigarette.

And the worse my relationship with cigarettes got, the more I wanted them. It was more than just a love affair – it was an obsession. Any vague fears I had about risks such as lung cancer were always overshadowed by the infinitely greater fear of never being able to smoke again. My cigarettes were part of my life. I needed them.

That was my affair with cigarettes, an affair that continued day and night, across jobs, events and 'life changes', an affair that lasted until I stumbled across a single scientific fact, a key piece of information about nicotine which fascinated me so much that I started to pull at it, like a thread in a jumper. I kept pulling... until the entire thing unravelled before my eyes and left me looking at the astonishing truth behind why smokers really smoke.

The result is the book you're now holding.

> **ANY VAGUE FEARS** I had about risks such as lung cancer were always overshadowed by the infinitely greater fear of never being able to smoke again.

Every day, I see thousands of smokers trapped inside cages, and most of them don't even know it. I see taxi drivers in cages, teenagers in cages, businessmen in cages, doctors in cages, mothers in cages, fathers in cages. I want all of them to escape, but I know it can't possibly happen. This year, more than a hundred thousand cigarette smokers in the UK will die, each of them helplessly trapped inside an invisible cage. Of course, their grieving families will blame cigarettes and smoking, but I know differently. I know what's really going to cause all these deaths: the fatal ignorance of a single fact, a fact so simple it could be written in the space occupied by the health warning on the front of a packet of cigarettes.

- **It's a fact that finally explains why ex-smokers who haven't smoked for twenty years can suddenly suffer from 'cravings' out of the blue.**

- **It's a fact that explains why hundreds of millions of non-smokers have smoked a single cigarette out of curiosity, without ever becoming hooked.**

- **It's a fact that explains why most smokers never escape from smoking for good, even if they get to the point where their lives have been made unbearable by cigarettes.**

Last night, I hosted a workshop for a small group of local smokers who were desperate to quit smoking, and who were absolutely convinced that they had already tried everything they could to stop.

Two of them had repeatedly attended a stop-smoking clinic that had 'disproved' all their reasons for smoking and explained that smoking a cigarette cannot give pleasure or relaxation, all it can do is briefly reduce the withdrawal symptoms caused by the previous cigarette. But *it still hadn't taken away their urge to smoke.* One of them had then spent more than a thousand pounds seeing a Harley Street hypnotist, without success.

There was a young woman who was desperate to stop smoking because she was training to compete in an 'Irish Dancing' competition, and cigarettes were ruining her fitness. There was a graphic designer in his early twenties whose chest had already reached the stage where he was coughing up blood each morning.

There were three women who work in a local property-letting agency. They'd decided to stop smoking together because they said they needed to give each other 'moral support'.

Then there was a quietly spoken Irish man I assumed was about sixty. He was smoking quietly and diligently while I spoke. He was rolling his own, using Old Holborn, the same tobacco I used to smoke during my 'roll-up phase'. I noticed that he rolled five cigarettes before lighting the first one. I also noticed that, during the first twenty minutes of the session, he smoked the first three cigarettes in rapid succession.

The smoking of his third cigarette coincided with me explaining how the unusual chemical properties of nicotine *trick the brains of smokers into misunderstanding what smoking a cigarette 'does'*. As I finished describing this fact and explaining what it means, his eyes lit up, and he started asking questions. This morning, he phoned to tell me he intends to contact every smoker he knows and tell them about the nicotine trick.

I hope he does. I can only tell so many people.

I don't know whether you're male or female, whether you're young or old. I don't know whether you smoke one cigarette each month or one hundred cigarettes every day. I don't know whether you smoked your first cigarette yesterday morning or sixty years ago. I don't know whether you inhale deeply, or whether you don't inhale at all.

IF YOU SMOKE cigarettes, I know why. And, whether you want to stop smoking or not, I'm going to explain the simple truth behind why you really smoke.

If you smoke cigarettes, I know why. And, whether you want to stop smoking or not, *I'm going to explain the simple truth behind why you really smoke*. So, let me start by telling you how you got where you are now. Let me explain exactly why you're here, now, reading a book about cigarettes and smoking.

Your Story

This is your story.

As a child, you were aware that some adults had a particular habit that made them put cigarettes in their mouths and light them. Then they did something that made smoke go all over the place. It looked like they were sucking the smoke into their lungs and breathing it out.

Maybe one or both of your parents had this habit, but that doesn't matter. What does matter is this. As a child, your mind was open, so smoking didn't seem particularly stupid, suicidal, addictive, antisocial or expensive. It was just something some adults 'did'.

Gradually, life forced you into the process known as 'growing up'. In order to start 'growing up', you looked at what your parents and other adults did, and you learned how to be like them. To start with, you learned to walk, by watching adults. Later, you learned to run, by watching adults. Then came more advanced skills, such as riding a bike, or using roller skates. Gradually, you learned social skills and, eventually, sexual skills. Some of this was instinctive, automatic, but even the instinctive skills were improved with practice.

It was all going so well…

… *then you learned how to smoke.*

At this point, let me make it clear that you didn't necessarily start smoking when you were very young. Some smokers start later in life, although this is usually the result of a trauma of some kind. The important point is that when you started smoking regularly, smoking quickly became as much a part of you as your other tastes, emotions, urges and instincts. In fact, *it became as much a part of you as your feelings towards your family and friends*, even though you didn't realise it at the time.

Now, at this second, I want you to think of someone you love. Do it right now. Bring their face into your mind. Remember one precious moment you've spent with them. Try to remember something specific, the sound of their voice or the way they smile. Take your time. Enjoy it for a few moments, then ask yourself a question:

What would happen if someone put a loaded gun against your head right now and threatened to pull the trigger unless you stopped loving this person?

Would you be able to do it?

No. You might be able to *say* you no longer loved them, but you wouldn't be able to make it happen.

Why not?

Because your emotions towards this person aren't deliberate or conscious. You don't have direct control over them, they're automatic, instinctive.

This means that no matter how much

pressure is put on you, you can't just turn these feelings off, even if your life depends upon it. It doesn't matter how hard you try, how dire the possible consequences, or even how much 'willpower' you use.

It just doesn't work like that.

So, this must mean that it's impossible to stop loving someone, right?

Wrong. It happens every day. Husbands fall out of love with wives, wives fall out of love with husbands, lifelong friends become enemies, or people simply drift apart.

This raises a confusing question. If it is possible to stop loving someone without even trying, why wouldn't you be able to do it with a gun pressed against your head? Why wouldn't you be able to do it even when your life depended on it?

Because you can only stop loving someone when you start to see them in a different way. Sometimes this happens gradually, and sometimes it happens in a single moment of realisation. But however it happens, you absolutely *cannot* make it happen just by trying.

You may not realise this, but I've just explained why you can't stop smoking cigarettes permanently by using 'willpower', or because it's

National Stop Smoking Day, or even *because you'll die if you don't stop*. And I haven't even mentioned cigarettes. Yet.

Every single year, millions of people try to do exactly what I've just described – they try to force themselves not to want their cigarettes any more. And every year most of them fail, even the ones who are already suffering life-threatening diseases through smoking. Without knowing it, they fail for exactly the reason I've just explained. So, before you even read another word of this book, I want you to do something for yourself, something that probably goes against every piece of advice you've ever been given. I want you to forget about 'stopping smoking'. It doesn't work like that. So relax and let me tell you how it does work.

> I WANT YOU to forget about 'stopping smoking'. It doesn't work like that. So relax and let me tell you how it does work.

Your Only Mistake

Have you ever leaned forward too quickly in the front seat of a car and inadvertently caused the seatbelt to lock? When this happens, you can't keep pushing, the seatbelt is too strong. In order to free yourself, you need to relax and lean, not *forwards*, but *backwards*.

Almost every smoker who wants to stop smoking is straining forwards against this invisible seatbelt. Their determination is undoing them because *every ounce of their strength is straining in the wrong direction*, making them feel overpowered and dejected. Even those smokers who claim to be happy are forced to live with the frightening suspicion that they couldn't stop smoking if they wanted to.

For almost twenty years, I was the same.

Whenever I talk to smokers who say they want to stop, my first priority is getting them to relax, something that is rarely their first instinct. The problem is, they think I'm going to somehow 'trick' them into parting with their cigarettes and this makes them anxious and stressed.

So, let me put your mind at ease right now. As much as this may surprise you, I'm not even going to suggest that you make a conscious decision to stop smoking. As you'll see shortly, it doesn't happen that way. In fact, neither you or I are going to make any decisions about whether you smoke or not. We're going to leave this decision to the part of your brain that keeps telling you to smoke, a part of you known as your *autonomic nervous system*, which I'm going to explain in detail later.

Throughout the rest of this book, I'm simply going to explain the truth behind why you really smoke, in straightforward, plain language. That's all. I'm not going to waste your time with endless anecdotes, or blow bubbles about how 'wonderful' it is to be a non-smoker. I haven't the slightest intention of turning you into a 'disciple' or 'convert'.

So lean back, forget about doing 'the right thing', and just do what your instincts tell you to do. And if those instincts tell you to grab a coffee, a cigarette and an ashtray, by all means do it, because, as a smoker, you're finally about to get some good news.

You're not selfish, you're not stupid and you're not weak-willed. All you did was make one mistake, the same one I made.

Maybe you think I'm talking about your first cigarette.

Actually, I'm not. Your first cigarette didn't do

the damage. You may be surprised to discover that almost all of the non-smokers you know have at some point smoked a single cigarette out of curiosity (if you don't believe me ask a few of them). And yet, they're not trapped where you are now. They're not reading a book about smoking and nicotine.

Why not?

Because the fatal mistake you made wasn't smoking your first cigarette. *It was smoking your second cigarette.* You'll see why later.

When you smoked your second cigarette, you began nothing less than an intimate relationship with cigarettes, a love-hate affair that you can't control, whether you think you can or not. You can't live with them, and you can't live without them. When you've got them, you sometimes wonder why you ever bothered, but when you haven't got them, you crave them so desperately that it borders on obsession.

THE ONLY REASON you've kept this affair going is because of a simple, fatal misunderstanding, a *chemical coincidence* that tricks part of your brain into making you light up again and again and again.

In fact, there are so many similarities

between smoking and having an ill-fated sexual affair that this book works precisely by making you see your cigarettes in this way. As soon as you understand why these similarities exist, you'll start to see your smoking in a way you never have before. You'll also see that the only reason you've kept this affair going is because of a simple, fatal misunderstanding, a *chemical coincidence* that tricks part of your brain into making you light up again and again and again.

But before I tell you about your affair with cigarettes started, let me tell you how my own affair started, how it went wrong, and how it was finally ended by a single piece of information.

Part One –
Pleasure

My Affair with Cigarettes

Like millions of smokers, I started smoking when I was still at school. The reasons are almost too boring to repeat. I wanted to appear adult, I wanted to seem clever and rebellious. I'm sure I don't need to spell out the way teenage boys see smoking.

By the time I was nineteen, I was smoking thirty roll-ups a day. At this point, I was working in a computer software company in a town called Altrincham, in Cheshire. It was by far the worst job I've ever had. I hated it. My task was to phone companies and arrange to send trial copies of software for them to load on their mainframe computers. It was tedious, mind-numbing work.

There were three of us doing the same job, and all of us were smokers. There was myself, a big ginger-haired lad called Tom, and a skinny bloke called Lee. We all smoked heavily. We were young male smokers. In our deluded minds, we were worldly and streetwise.

Of course, even though I chose to smoke, several times each day my body helpfully reminded me that it was time for me to exercise my 'choice' as a smoker. It was the same with my two smoking friends. So, just like every other smoker on the planet, we quietly created a schedule of smoking 'breaks' that allowed us to satisfy these desires. None of us ever mentioned 'addiction', 'dependence' or 'withdrawal symptoms'.

> OF COURSE, EVEN though I chose to smoke, several times each day my body helpfully reminded me that it was time for me to exercise my 'choice' as a smoker.

Several times each day, we would head up to the rooftop car park, for our little 'treat'. At the time, these breaks seemed to serve two purposes. The first was the cigarette itself. I enjoyed smoking, it used to relax me. It never occurred to me to wonder why I *needed* to relax thirty times each day (when most non-smokers seemed to be relaxed anyway). I just accepted that this was how cigarettes 'worked'.

The second purpose was that it made me feel I was rebelling against the lousy company I worked for, and the idiotic egomaniac who ran it. I saw myself as rebellious, sticking my middle finger up at authority, and doing my own thing. I believed I was showing my independence.

By the time I reached my late twenties, my smoking had endowed me with three sparkling and wondrous gifts, gifts that my non-smoking friends never enjoyed. Let me tell you about them.

The first gift was an impressively waxy complexion, which was suspiciously similar to Plasticine. Even on the occasions when I had what passed for a 'suntan', I could always see the grey skin underneath.

The second gift was a spectacular inability to run more than sixty yards without collapsing. On one occasion, I 'sprinted' for a bus, only to miss it by less than five seconds. For a minute or so, I stood, like a broken toilet, in full view of the passing traffic. Unfortunately, rather than recovering manfully, I collapsed forwards and knocked two of my front teeth loose on the pavement. When I finally managed to get back on my feet, I was then subjected to the unique and shattering indignity of having an old lady help *me* across the road, back towards where I lived.

The third and final gift was a smoker's cough so rasping and loud that I sounded like a gannet hatchery whenever I tried to clear my throat (which was most of the time). I also started to make a strange, low-pitched wheezing sound whenever I was trying to sleep, a sound caused by the effects of cigarette smoke on the linings of my nose and throat.

During this time, I made dozens of 'attempts' to stop smoking, but none of them ever lasted very long. They were usually triggered by the consequences of a heavy night in the pub, and the feeling of being choked and polluted the next morning. In most cases, I was back smoking like a chimney within a day or so. I always assumed that the 'habit' was simply too strong for my mind to let go of. But it didn't matter too much to me at that point. I was still only young. I had years, if not decades, to quit if I wanted to.

So I carried on smoking.

Unfortunately, my blissful affair with cigarettes

was rudely interrupted one day in 1998. It was the day a close friend, a smoker in his late thirties, was diagnosed with small cell lung carcinoma, the most virulent form of lung cancer. Over a period of months, I watched him shrink to nothing before he died.

On the day of his funeral, I was frightened and shocked. To make matters worse, for some reason I smoked more than fifty cigarettes during the day. It was as though each cigarette wasn't working, but I still needed to keep lighting another one and another one. By the end of the day I felt as though my entire body was saturated with nicotine.

The next morning, I decided to stop smoking for good. I felt sure that this attempt wasn't going to be like my earlier, half-hearted efforts. *It was going to be serious this time*. It didn't even occur to me that it might be difficult. But when I tried, I was horrified to discover that *it wasn't just difficult, but impossible*.

By the end of the first day I was sweating and my hands were shaking. I couldn't concentrate on anything. That first night, I kept waking up, shaken and distressed. The following morning, it seemed like my entire body was screaming for a cigarette. I lasted just one more day before smoking again.

I was horrified. I honestly couldn't believe it. I'd heard other smokers talking about being 'nicotine addicts', but the phrase had never rung true with me. It always sounded much too dramatic. Addiction was for winos and drop-outs. I wasn't an addict. I was a smoker.

But I knew something was wrong, and I was scared. Scared of smoking, and even more scared of quitting.

Reluctantly, I bought a book on how to stop smoking, but I was soon put off by its self-righteous tone and by the sheer number of pages. Determined to give it a chance, I persevered, only to find that it also seemed to contradict itself. For instance, it began by claiming that smokers' bodies never crave nicotine, but it later stated over and over again that my body would continue to 'crave nicotine' for several days after my final cigarette! Totally confused, I phoned one of the clinics on which the book was based,

THE FOLLOWING MORNING, it seemed like my entire body was screaming for a cigarette. I lasted just one more day before smoking again.

only to be advised that it would all be explained much better if I came to a clinic instead!

So I decided to help myself. I created a set of 'hint cards' containing useful pieces of information reminding myself of the reasons not to smoke. I started getting contributions from other smokers I knew who were trying to stop. It was bizarre, at one stage it reminded me of those swap cards at school:

'Have you got *Smoking Damages Your Arteries?*'

'No. I'll swap you for *Smoking Isn't Cool Any More.*'

Within a few months, these cards became a book called *The Little Book Of Not Smoking*, a book that surprised me by not only getting published, but by becoming very successful. Shortly afterwards, I was contacted by *The Times*, who wanted to use the book as part of their *Stop Smoking For The Millennium* feature. I was even interviewed by the BBC about my views on smoking and nicotine.

I must confess that, at the time, I felt out of my depth. Sure, the book was helpful in giving people reasons for stopping smoking, and it contained a lot of useful information, but it didn't explain the million-dollar questions of *why people smoke*, or *where 'cravings' come from.* The simple truth is, I didn't know the answer to these questions then. But, with the success of the book, I suddenly had access to more information, more experts, and most importantly of all – more smokers.

The twelve months that followed were the most amazing of my entire life. Slowly and obsessively, I investigated every conceivable method of stopping smoking, including hypnosis, acupuncture, aversion therapy, videos, willpower, nicotine patches, clinics, books, support groups, Nicotine Anonymous, *everything*. I spoke to hundreds of smokers and ex-smokers about the methods they'd used (or tried to use) to stop smoking. I spoke to smokers who'd only just started, and I spoke to people who were literally dying from smoking.

AT LAST, I had access to genuine scientific information. I settled down to some serious reading. Almost immediately, I started to uncover some extremely surprising facts.

During the first half of 2000, I started to dig even deeper. I got hold of scientific reports going back decades, including UK government white papers and reports by the World Health Organization and the US Surgeon General, as well as scientific documents from the tobacco industry. I contacted experts in the subjects of nicotine, tobacco and drug addiction. I examined every scientific detail of how nicotine affects the brain, the specifics of 'nicotinic receptor sites', 'dopamine pathways' and the intricate mechanics of how the body reacts to cigarette smoke. I carefully compared the recorded effects of nicotine to the effects of other drugs such as alcohol, cocaine and heroin.

At last, I had access to genuine scientific information. I settled down to some serious reading. Almost immediately, I started to uncover some extremely surprising facts.

For instance:

- **Did you know that laboratory studies have failed to detect any mood enhancing effects of smoking or nicotine?**

- **Did you know that the first drag on each cigarette you smoke is taken differently from all the others that follow?**

- **Did you know that nicotine is even more poisonous than arsenic or strychnine?**

I didn't. This information was strangely missing from most of the books I'd read. At this point, I need to say a special thank-you to ASH. As you may know, ASH (Action on Smoking and Health) is an organisation that is famous for attacking the activities of the tobacco industry. It was ASH's UK director, Clive Bates, who first told me about the extensive report on smoking and nicotine carried out by the Royal College of Physicians, a source of information that has been absolutely crucial in writing this book.

As I studied this report (and many others), the overall picture gradually started to become much clearer. But one thing still worried me. Even while I was slowly piecing together the true picture of nicotine and smoking, I still seemed to be suffering from occasional withdrawal symptoms of my own, even such a long time after stopping. The curious thing was, *on some days the temptation to smoke was absolute hell, and on other days I wouldn't notice a thing.* This never struck me as being strange. I just assumed that withdrawal symptoms from any drug

> THE CURIOUS THING was, on some days the temptation to smoke was absolute hell, and on other days I wouldn't notice a thing.

worked in the same way – that they come and go at random.

I was wrong. As I now know, the reason I was suffering at random times was simple: it wasn't withdrawal symptoms I was suffering from at all. And soon afterwards, I finally stumbled across what was really happening.

What I uncovered is, quite simply, the core reason behind why most smokers can't stop smoking, no matter how hard they try. In fact, it explains why, in most cases, *the more determined you are to stop smoking, the more impossible it is*.

It also finally explains one of the biggest mysteries of smoking, the bizarre phenomenon that has demoralised more ex-smokers than anything else: how 'cravings' can suddenly strike out of the blue even years after you've stopped smoking!

The real reason that millions of smokers can't escape is based on nothing less than *a simple coincidence relating to the delayed effects of nicotine*, a coincidence that 'tricks' the brains of smokers into making a *fatal wrong connection* each time they smoke, a connection that keeps them lighting up whether they want to or not, even when they know it's killing them, *a connection that is made without them ever being consciously aware of it.*

I soon realised that every time I'd ever wanted to smoke, the impulse had been based on this single misunderstanding. Of course, the *results* of smoking each cigarette had been anything but a misunderstanding. The consequences had been real, the smell, the cost, the hacking cough, the splitting headaches, the stained teeth, all of that had been real.

But the reason for smoking the cigarette had been based on an astonishing piece of self-deception, a bizarre, chemically induced illusion: the nicotine trick.

This simple piece of self-deception will be explained in its own chapter. At this point, please do not jump straight to this chapter. You'll see why shortly.

> I SOON REALISED that every time I'd ever wanted to smoke, the impulse had been based on this single misunderstanding.

Having discovered how nicotine 'tricks' the brains of smokers, I spent several days trying to digest exactly what it meant. When it finally clicked, it seemed as though a movie suddenly started playing inside my head, a movie comprising every cigarette I'd ever smoked. Each scene was identical to the way it had happened in real life, with one difference: just before I lit each cigarette, a barely visible shadow appeared over my shoulder and seemed to whisper something into my ear, something that made the cigarette 'work'.

I now know that every smoker has this shadow following them around

I NOW KNOW that every smoker has this shadow following them around until they finish with their cigarettes… or until their cigarettes finish with them.

until they finish with their cigarettes… or until their cigarettes finish with them. Each time you light a cigarette, you do it *because this shadow has stepped up behind you and whispered a sweet deception into your ear, a single, poisonous lie.*

When I finally understood precisely how smoking 'worked', I was able to develop a simple technique to switch my cravings off (I'll show you how later), and they haven't come back at any point since. It doesn't make any difference what I do or where I go. I can drink alcohol, go to weddings or funerals, hang around with smokers, and still feel absolutely no inclination to smoke.

Cigarettes, quite simply, don't work for me anymore.

I now know that the only way I could ever start smoking again would be by allowing myself to be professionally hypnotised and tricked into misunderstanding the 'feeling' of smoking in the way I used to – and in the way you almost certainly do now.

Soon after discovering the nicotine trick, I started explaining it to other smokers. A few of them stopped smoking soon afterwards; others didn't. The ones who did stop were a source of tremendous pride and pleasure to me. By simply giving a piece of information to them and explaining what it really meant, I'd been able to completely unlock their fascination with cigarettes, allowing them to walk away from the whispering shadow on their shoulder, into bright sunshine.

But the ones who carried on smoking, they worried me. How could they possibly continue to smoke after what I'd told them?

I soon realised why. Although they'd accepted the information at a conscious level, something had prevented them from adopting it at a deeper, emotional level.

They understood it, but they didn't 'get it'.

Have you ever tried to make someone listen to a piece of music that you think is the most jaw-dropping song you've ever heard, only to have them say something like, '... *yeah. That guitar bit at the beginning is quite clever...*'

... and you just know they haven't got it, *they haven't really got it like you've got it*?

I have. I once persuaded someone to listen to my all-time favourite piece of music, a song called 'Shine On You Crazy Diamond' by Pink Floyd, a song so inspired and heart-rending that I've probably listened to it ten thousand times. She listened to it politely, but didn't 'get it' on the first listening.

She later told me that she'd listened to it again by herself a few days afterwards and it had suddenly got to her. This is what happens with the reason people really smoke, the nicotine trick. By itself, it's just an interesting coincidence about nicotine, a simple fact that, as a smoker, you'll know is true as soon as I tell you what it is. But that won't mean you've 'got it' and that's what the final chapter of this book is for. It's to make sure that this fact sinks deep into your mind and becomes part of you, just like your favourite song. When this finally happens, you will be less tempted to smoke than someone who's never touched a cigarette in their entire life.

A DESTRUCTIVE RELATIONSHIP

During the first few months of the nicotine trick, I realised that it was taking more than two hours to explain to smokers why they really smoke. This was because, although the nicotine trick itself only takes a few minutes to explain, smokers always ask a lot of other questions, such as...

'What will I replace smoking with?'

'When will the cravings go?'

'Should I avoid pubs and other smokers while I'm trying to stop smoking?'

'What should I do to help myself concentrate?'

'Will I put on weight?'

When I realised that most smokers have these questions and more, I started looking for a way of explaining the nicotine trick that would answer these questions at the same time, a familiar concept that smokers could immediately relate to at an emotional level.

I found it by chance, in a woman I'll call

Charlene, a stressed-out smoker whom I met through one of her work colleagues. Charlene was a sales rep working for a computer company, and she was one of the heaviest smokers I've ever met. She was only twenty-eight at the time, although she openly complained about looking ten years older because of the effects of smoking. Even at such a young age, she already had the dry hair, damaged skin and milky eyes of the truly chronic smoker.

I STARTED LOOKING for a way of explaining the nicotine trick that would answer these questions at the same time, a familiar concept that smokers could immediately relate to at an emotional level.

Charlene had absolutely no intention of stopping smoking. When I first asked her why she smoked, she insisted that she 'enjoyed it', and refused to discuss the matter further. I didn't push, because I never try to persuade people to stop smoking. But it was obvious that Charlene was desperately unhappy and worried about the effects smoking was having on her looks and health.

Over a period of weeks, I explained the nicotine trick to a number of Charlene's smoking friends, two of whom stopped smoking, easily and painlessly. This made Charlene inquisitive and, gradually, she started to open up about what seemed to trigger her cravings.

It emerged that Charlene was unhappily involved in an affair with someone where she worked, a married man who publicly treated her with contempt, and who often ridiculed her behind her back. Charlene openly admitted that her feelings of anger and rejection would very often explode in the office. Each time she had a blazing row with her boyfriend, she would storm outside and smoke a cigarette, or sometimes two.

I asked her why she was driven to poison herself with cigarette smoke every time her boyfriend let her down. She said,

'Well at least cigarettes don't treat me like ****!'

By uttering those words, Charlene made me realise that the relationship smokers have with cigarettes isn't really physical – it's emotional. I also realised that smoking is exactly the same as the pointless and one-sided affair Charlene was involved in: it's a relationship based on betrayal, deception, illusion… and disappointment.

As soon as I realised this, I suddenly had a new way of explaining the nicotine trick to smokers, a way that explains your relationship with cigarettes as an *obsessive sexual affair*. As you're about to discover, by seeing smoking in this way, you'll find it easy to understand the real truth behind the way cigarettes make you feel. You'll see:

- **How you've done all the work right from the start.**

- **How part of your brain has been tricked into 'faking' pleasure when you smoke.**

- **Why it hurts so much to see someone else 'enjoying' a cigarette after you've stopped smoking.**

* * * * *

In 2001, I started organising small workshops at a local community centre, in which I spoke to groups of smokers directly. Almost all of these people had read at least one book on how to stop smoking. Some smokers even brought these books with them, probably hoping they would act like some sort of lucky charm. Strangely, many people who came to workshops had successfully stopped smoking by using stop-smoking books, but at some point the effect had 'worn off' and they'd started smoking again.

One thing that took me by surprise was the fact that, each time I spoke to a group of smokers, even the quiet ones seemed absolutely hell-bent on telling me why they smoked, why they found it so hard to give up, their thoughts on whether smoking is habit or drug addiction (it's neither, as you'll soon see), and so on.

AS SOON AS I realised this, I suddenly had a new way of explaining the nicotine trick to smokers, a way that explains your relationship with cigarettes as an obsessive sexual affair.

To start with, I couldn't understand why smokers were so insistent on telling me (and each other) their opinions on smoking in such detail. Surely I was there to explain it to them, not the other way round? I now realise that smokers do this not because they want to argue or interrupt, but because *they desperately want to believe that they're in control of their relationship with cigarettes*.

When I was a smoker, I was the same, totally determined to believe that I was in control, even though my reason for smoking mysteriously changed every few years. First it was *to appear adult and sophisticated*, then it was *because I enjoyed it*, and eventually it was *because I couldn't quit*.

The real problem was that until I eventually stumbled across the nicotine trick, I never realised that my real reason for keeping the affair going didn't exist in my conscious mind, so I was never able to do anything about it.

But that's enough about me. Now you know how this book came about, let's talk about you. If you're ever going to end your affair with cigarettes, you need to know why you started it in the first place.

Your Affair with Cigarettes

You can't have an affair unless something starts it. So let's look at how your affair with cigarettes began.

First of all, let's be clear on exactly what I mean by an 'affair', as opposed to a normal, healthy relationship. For the purposes of this, let's say that, in order for a relationship to be an affair, it needs to be three things. It needs to be *painful*, it needs to involve *deceit*, and it needs to have *no future*. Smoking matches all three of these criteria handsomely. Let's see why.

I assume that you don't need an explanation of why smoking is painful. But let's look at the most extreme example of how painful smoking can be – lung cancer.

If you smoke, maybe you take the view that lung cancer is simply an 'occupational hazard', or just one of those tired statistics rolled out each year by all the anti-smoking 'talking heads' who seem so desperate to get their faces on television every National Stop Smoking Day. Maybe you don't plan to get lung cancer. If so, let me tell you about a friend of mine who had a plan.

He's called Dave, and he's a train driver. Even without me giving his surname, I'm sure Dave would want me to point out that he's not just any old train driver. He drives the Inter-City trains, the fast ones. By the time you read this, he may have achieved his lifetime's ambition of driving the high-speed 'Euro-Star' trains to Paris.

Dave was a heavy smoker until I got to him almost by mistake with a single, little-known fact, a dirty little secret that *the cigarette companies have kept carefully hidden from smokers*. It wasn't the nicotine trick itself, it was something else, something deeply unpleasant.

Before I tell you what this secret is, let me tell

you about Dave's plan. Dave's father, a smoker, died of lung cancer in his fifties. Dave had been smoking since he was fifteen, and he'd calculated that, even if he smoked until he was forty, he'd still be able to stop and 'probably not get lung cancer'.

He thought he'd figured out a way in which he could smoke without it catching him out.

> DAVE WAS A heavy smoker until I got to him almost by mistake with a single, little-known fact, a dirty little secret that the cigarette companies have kept carefully hidden from smokers.

Maybe you're expecting me to rant about how stupid, irresponsible and suicidal Dave's plan was. Maybe you think I'd be right if I did. Actually, many smokers I help do have a masochistic desire for me to do exactly this, but I never indulge it and I never will.

Here's why. Every smoker in the world has a similar plan. I had one. You've got one. Maybe you don't think you've got a plan. Maybe you just want to read this book and 'see how it goes'. Maybe you're waiting for a train and flicking through this book in the bookshop. Maybe you're just one of these 'naturally curious types'.

But whatever you think, you don't plan to

keep smoking until you get lung cancer. And if you don't plan to do that, it means you do plan to avoid it happening, which means you have got a plan. You just can't quite figure out how to implement it – or *when*.

Let me tell you something else. The cigarette companies figured this out decades ago. Why else do you think every tobacconist, newsagent and garage sells cigarettes in packets of *ten* as well as packets of twenty? Do you really think it's because smokers can't afford twenty cigarettes?

No. Smokers will always find the money for cigarettes (as you and I well know).

Do you think it's because of the discreet, convenient size? Hardly. Any pretence of convenience will be blown away as soon as the packet is opened and there's a handful of cellophane and foil to dispose of. And any pretence of discretion will be blown away by the first stinking blast of smoke.

In fact, the real reason cigarettes are sold in tens is because millions of smokers are so utterly depressed by the fact that they smoke, that they don't even want to consider the idea of being forced to smoke another twenty cigarettes. Maybe just another ten cigarettes will finally satisfy whatever it is they need satisfying, so they can stop.

But does it work? Does ten more cigarettes finally kill the urge? Does it hit the spot once and for all?

Does it finally 'do it for you'?

No, which means that *each cigarette is somehow creating a need for more cigarettes*, a fact that, even by itself, suggests that smoking can't be driven by pleasure. After all, when you've watched your favourite film, does it immediately create a desperate need to watch it all over again? No. That would be ridiculous, wouldn't it? But that's the point – I've already explained that your relationship with cigarettes is an affair, and how many affairs do you know of that are based on logic and common sense?

Anyway, let me tell you what I told Dave. It was a piece of information revealed by a former US Surgeon General. It's this. Tobacco is grown in soil that is rich in phosphates. As a result, cigarette smoke contains a chemical called polonium-210.

Big deal, right?

Except that polonium-210 is *radioactive*. It forms radiation 'hot spots' in living lung tissue, areas of infected tissue which then slowly become cancerous tumours. When I told Dave this, his face went grey. In fact, let me be more specific. Dave's face went *more grey* (as a heavy smoker, his face was already grey).

I was surprised that this fact made Dave so upset, because I hadn't even bothered to mention it to anyone else. I asked him why it made any difference *how* cigarettes cause lung cancer. He told me it was just the *idea* of breathing radioactive metals directly into his chest. It just somehow seemed worse, more obscene, *more suicidal than the idea of black tar*.

THE TRUTH IS, the tar in cigarettes is carcinogenic, but the radiation from the polonium is the real killer.

The truth is, the tar in cigarettes *is* carcinogenic, but the radiation from the polonium is the real killer. Scientists have estimated that, in just one year, a forty-a-day smoker is exposed to the radiation equivalent of *hundreds of chest x-rays*. Incidentally, if this fact has actually made you want to light a cigarette right now, don't worry. When you understand what nicotine really does, you'll know exactly why this happens, and how to make it stop.

THREE STRIKES AND YOU'RE OUT

Okay, so if you're destined to get lung cancer from smoking, it probably won't be from the tar. It will be from the radiation. But, however you get it… *do you know how someone with lung cancer actually dies?*

In fact, the pain of lung cancer arrives in three instalments. The first part is the physical agony of the disease itself. When tumours start growing inside your lungs, they slowly rip apart the most tender and sensitive tissue in your entire body. I'm told that the pain is almost impossible to describe. Some days it feels like a dull ache. On other days, it feels like hot coals deep inside your chest.

And consider this. If your leg is broken, you can rest it while it gets better, you can ease the pressure on it by lying down, or by using crutches, or by using a wheelchair, or whatever. You can give it time to get better.

Not with lung cancer. You can't just stop breathing, or you'll die. So you're forced to keep stretching tissue that is now riddled with dark growths, growths that will probably break up and travel round the rest of your body. This is called *metastasis*. When this happens, it's a lottery (without the possibility of winning anything) as to which part of you gets cancer next. If you're female, it could be your cervix or your breasts. If you're male, it could be your testicles or penis.

Whether you're male or female, it could be your brain, your stomach, your bowels, your kidneys or your liver. It could be your throat. Have you ever seen those ex-smokers who now need a hole in their neck to breathe? Enough said.

And the real pain hasn't even started yet. This is just the first instalment.

The second part is the treatment. It may involve chemotherapy, in which case you'll be pumped full of chemicals that will kill healthy tissue as well as (hopefully) some cancer cells. Even if your body tries to reject the chemicals, you'll be told to continue.

When I was about seven, a woman who lived round the corner got lung cancer from smoking. I can still remember her. She was called Jane. She had blue eyes and long brown hair. She used to babysit for me and my younger brother. Then she got sick and I heard my parents talking about smoking and lung cancer. I heard the word *chemotherapy* and it terrified me. I knew there was something about the word, something that sounded like death.

I only saw Jane one more time. I was riding my bike, and she was being driven back to her house from the hospital. No one told me that the treatment had failed and she'd come home to die. It was a hot, sunny day, but she was wearing what looked like a white balaclava. I asked my mother why she was wearing it. She gave some unlikely explanation to avoid scaring me. Years later, I discovered that, in addition to the chemotherapy, Jane had been given radiation therapy, which had caused all her hair to fall out.

More radiation to add to the radiation from the cigarettes she'd smoked.

Then there's the most agonising pain of all. The pain of your family and friends being forced to watch you die, eaten up from the inside. Worse still, it's not as though you're dying because you're a hero or because you've been mortally injured trying to save someone's life. You're dying because you smoked cigarettes. You're lying in a hospital bed, with a hissing oxygen canister next to you, asking yourself one question:

'What did I do wrong?'

So, before it gets that far, let's ask this question right now. What did you do wrong? The answer, like the question itself, is painfully simple:

Not much.

You made one fatal mistake, which was smoking your second cigarette. And you might now be heading towards an agonising death, simply because this single mistake led you into the path of a strange chemical coincidence called *the nicotine trick*, a coincidence that caused your brain to make a fatal wrong connection, a crossed wire that has forced you to smoke again and again and again.

THEN THERE'S THE most agonising pain of all. The pain of your family and friends being forced to watch you die, eaten up from the inside.

Some smokers object to other people using the word 'forced'. They don't like the implication that they don't choose to smoke. I don't blame them. Nevertheless, 'forced' is the right word. Let me prove it. If you were walking along the pavement and a car suddenly veered off the road towards you, part of your brain would force you to jump out of the way, wouldn't it?

Well, believe it or not, *the mechanism that*

makes this happen is exactly the same mechanism that makes you light a cigarette, which is why you always want to smoke in stressful situations. By the end of this book, you'll know exactly how it works. There won't be a single element of doubt or confusion, which means that, even if you decide to keep smoking for the rest of your life, *you'll finally be doing it in full possession of the facts.*

DECEIT

Remember what I said about affairs? They're painful and have no future. But that wasn't all. I also mentioned that your affair with cigarettes involves deceit.

You may find this offensive. You should. It is offensive, but look at the facts. Have you always been totally honest about how many cigarettes you smoke? Or have you conveniently 'forgotten' those extra fags you borrowed, or that extra pack you got at the airport, or the few home-made ones you rolled from that pouch of tobacco that you inadvertently bought when you couldn't get any ordinary cigarettes. (Not that you were desperate, of course. You just enjoy smoking, and it's perfectly natural to go into a blind panic when you can't do something you 'enjoy', isn't it?)

Have you ever smoked in someone's bathroom and then denied it so passionately that even *you* started to believe you hadn't done it? Did you really think you got away with it? Have you any idea what a bathroom smells like to a non-smoker after someone's smoked in it? Do you really believe that any amount of air freshener or bathroom deodorant can mask the smell of cigarette smoke?

If so, I have disturbing news. *The smell has a half-life of about twenty years and you couldn't wash it off the face of a diamond.*

I once smoked a cigarette in the kitchen of a friend's flat while he went out to get some Chinese food. When I realised how bad the smell was, I opened the kitchen window, allowing a force-ten gale to blow my cigarettes straight off the table and behind the oven, from where they had to be retrieved by my friend when he got back.

And I still denied I'd smoked in his kitchen.

What about the effects of cigarettes on your health? Have you been honest with yourself about those? Have you blamed that mysterious chest pain on stress, or caffeine, or a trapped nerve (in your chest? Don't laugh. I once claimed it as an excuse). Have you put your creeping lack of fitness, shortage of breath and slug-like posture down to the normal wear and tear of a life in the 'fast lane'? Have you put your waxy complexion and dull eyes down to the fact that you've not had a holiday

WHAT ABOUT THE effects of cigarettes on your health? Have you been honest with yourself about those?

for a while? Whenever you've been asked how many you smoke, have you ever corrected the amount upwards, or always downwards? In fact, have you ever heard anyone proudly declare themselves to be a sixty-a-day smoker?

If you have, it's an act, believe me.

I met one of these people a little while ago, while I was about to start a nicotine trick workshop. He intercepted me on my way in, and loudly declared that he was proud to be a heavy smoker. I told him I respected his honesty. An hour later, he was begging me to explain the nicotine trick to him.

Proud to be a smoker? Get real.

You can't have an affair without lying. It comes with the territory. I once went to a hypnotist to help me stop smoking. He charged me so much money that it made it impossible for me to afford any more cigarettes for a while, but it had no effect on my actual smoking. I've often wondered whether his 'relaxation' techniques worked better on my wallet than they did on my subconscious mind. Fortunately, I had an 'emergency cigarette' in my jacket, which I smoked on the way home from his clinic. When I got home, my father asked me if it had worked, and I said yes, honestly meaning it, and believing that the hypnosis just needed time to 'kick in' (which it never did).

But the deceit isn't all one way. Your cigarettes have deceived you too.

You've probably heard stories about someone deliberately infecting others with AIDS, by starting sexual affairs with them. Can you imagine falling for someone who would use the moment of maximum intimacy to infect you with a fatal disease?

You don't need to imagine it. Every cigarette you've ever smoked has betrayed you in exactly this way. You're having an affair with someone who is now going to kill you, if you let them.

You think this is overly dramatic? Consider the facts. Most women who are killed by violent partners have been attacked many times before the fatal attack. Millions of people stay in abusive relationships simply because they think they 'deserve it'.

What about you? Do you think you deserve 'everything you get' from smoking? Do you believe you've done something bad enough to die for?

You'd be amazed at how many smokers do.

But I wasn't one of them. I wasn't prepared to die for my smoking, which is why I dedicated myself to researching every single piece of scientific information ever recorded on nicotine until I found the answer. I didn't expect to find it inside a single fact, but even if the answer had been long and convoluted, I still would have found it eventually.

> I WASN'T PREPARED to die for my smoking, which is why I dedicated myself to researching every single piece of scientific information ever recorded on nicotine until I found the answer.

I won't lay down my life just so that the faceless suits who run the tobacco industry can put another few million dollars into their offshore investment portfolios. And I won't let you lose your life for them either, if I can help it.

THE START OF YOUR AFFAIR

Okay. Now we know what your affair *is*, let's look at the point in question – how it started.

How does *any* affair start? There are actually three main ways:

- **It can start because you're bored.**

- **It can start because it seems adult and exciting.**

- **It can start because you're unhappy and lonely.**

For me, it was the second reason. I smoked to fit in. As a schoolboy, I was short, skinny, round-shouldered, forcibly well groomed and, as such, highly unimpressive. Worse still, I was good at lessons, but bad at football and *hopeless* at fighting. As a result, every attempt I made to deviously infiltrate the 'in-crowd' was met with hostility, scorn, and on occasion, violence.

But dire situations call for dire measures, and the only thing I could think of was smoking.

I remember my first cigarette. It was a bitterly cold morning. The older boys I was trying to befriend had rolled one for me, and were watching my attempts with smirking, predatory interest. I was wary of its contents, terrified of its creators, but desperate not to fail. I smoked it in front of them. I was dizzy, sick and shaking, but I still did it, because I wanted to belong, to be 'cool'.

That was the reason I smoked my first cigarette.

But, as I now know, I smoked my second cigarette for a completely different reason. And as soon as I took the first drag on the second cigarette… deep inside my brain, a fatal wrong connection was made, a connection based on a simple chemical coincidence called the nicotine trick. As a result, I was hooked. My affair with cigarettes had started.

What about you? Did you start smoking to 'fit in'? Were you taken in by the image of confidence and sophistication that seems to be associated with cigarettes? If so, you're in good company. Most smokers start for this reason.

But be honest – does smoking *still* seem grown-up and sophisticated to you? Do you really feel attractive or mature with a cigarette between your lips? Or does it now seem weak, sad, pathetic and childish? After all, you don't still dress or act like you did when you first started smoking, do you? Haven't you matured since then? Haven't you got rid of most of the silly habits that you had as a teenager?

WHAT ABOUT YOU?
Did you start smoking to 'fit in'? Were you taken in by the image of confidence and sophistication that seems to be associated with cigarettes?

So, why not smoking?

Because, as anyone who understands nicotine will tell you, smoking is not just a habit.

Of course, the cigarette companies will always do what they can to trick people into starting affairs with smoking. They do this in some truly terrifying ways, most of which are beyond the scope of this book. During my research into the nicotine trick, I was fortunate to come into contact with Jim Hagart, a chartered psychologist and lecturer who just happens to be one of the world's leading experts in subliminal advertising techniques. Jim's articles are essential reading for anyone wanting to know how cigarette advertising can actually trick your brain into craving cigarettes.

Back to your affair with cigarettes. Maybe it started like mine, because you wanted to appear adult and sophisticated. But sometimes people start smoking for another reason. I've lost count of the smokers who tell me they started smoking at *funerals*. In fact, I met one very recently. I asked him if he'd ever smoked *before* the funeral. He said no. I asked what had made him want to smoke at a funeral. (I knew the answer in advance, but people absorb information better if they hear it from themselves.) He said he was upset and wanted something to calm him. I asked whether it had. He explained that the first one was awful, but that the second one seemed to relax him slightly. I asked him if he had any idea why this might be, and he said he hadn't. Within six months of the funeral, this man's guilty affair with cigarettes had turned into a forty-a-day nightmare. He was desperate to escape but frightened of what to expect.

Incidentally, never forget that fear is infinitely more powerful than any drug. If you believe in voodoo magic, it can actually be used to kill you. If you believe in ghosts, they can haunt you. In both cases, the damage is being done not by knowledge, but by fear and confusion. And let's be honest – when it comes to stopping smoking, what are you supposed to think? There are so many people trying to tell you how difficult it is to stop smoking, how can anyone blame you for being anxious and confused?

I don't blame you. The nicotine trick scared me half to death until I discovered how it worked.

Have you ever noticed that sexual affairs are often based on having a twisted view of someone, a view that other people sometimes can't understand? Have you ever had a friend excitedly tell you about someone fantastically sexy and attractive they've discovered, and then been forced to keep a straight face when you finally met them?

You may grin at the image, but behind my apparent flippancy is a dead serious message. The only thing that prevents you from ending your affair with your cigarettes is your own twisted view of smoking.

But, at this point, I can hardly blame you for this, because I've still not explained *why* it's twisted, have I? So let's move on. It's time to talk about the subject of your affair.

Your Bed Partner

If you absorb the contents of this book, you'll lose interest in your cigarettes, no matter how long you've been smoking, no matter how many cigarettes you smoke, no longer how many attempts you've made to stop smoking in the past. Whether you find this statement unbelievable or not makes no difference. If someone gives you a piece of information that makes it impossible for you to maintain the same view of something, that view changes whether you want it to or not.

This is what will happen to the relationship between you and your cigarettes.

At this point, don't waste your time mentally dragging up the desperate lengths you've gone to in the past trying to stop smoking, or the miserable ex-smokers you know who tell you they still get withdrawal symptoms years later, or the fact that you were forced to sheepishly ask for your money back after attending a stop-smoking clinic six times. None of that is relevant, and none of it will make the slightest difference to the outcome. The outcome of reading this book will be that your attraction to cigarettes will fade, seemingly by itself.

> THE ONLY THING that prevents you from ending your affair with your cigarettes is your own twisted view of smoking.

How can I be so sure?

Because I'm about to explain exactly what smoking a cigarette really 'does', and I'm going to explain it in such detail that *the part of your brain that makes you smoke* will be unable to hide from the truth. When this happens, it will be like a cut nerve starting to die. You won't need to *try* to lose interest in smoking, because your affair with cigarettes is actually based on such a simple illusion that it will completely cease to impress you as soon as I explain it in detail.

YOUR AFFAIR WITH cigarettes is actually based on such a simple illusion that it will completely cease to impress you as soon as I explain it in detail.

Have you ever seen the TV programme *Magic's Greatest Secrets Revealed*? It's an American programme in which a masked 'magician' first executes some of the most famous magic tricks in the world, ranging from the tedious (card tricks) all the way to the potentially expensive (making jet airliners disappear).

Having executed each trick exactly as it would be seen by an audience, the masked magician then slowly goes through the trick again from scratch, and explains how it's done, exposing every piece of deception upon which the trick is built. When I first sat down to watch it, I was expecting to see an incredible and ingenious solution for each illusion.

I was disappointed.

Time after time, I watched as the most fantastic and baffling of tricks proved to have a mundane and disappointing explanation, one that suddenly seemed incredibly obvious as soon as the trick was shown again:

- **The woman who 'disappears' is crouched behind a base that suddenly seems unnecessarily deep.**

- **The 'vanishing' plane never goes anywhere. The camera is on a revolving pedestal the entire time.**

- **The bullet 'caught' in the teeth is already there. The glass plate through which it was 'fired' was shattered by a remote-controlled charge.**

It all seems so obvious afterwards, doesn't it? But once you've seen the secret of how a magic trick works, how fascinating is it? How amazing does it now seem? How keen are you to see it again?

Very shortly, I'll reveal smoking's greatest secret, the nicotine trick. And your cigarettes will start to lose their attraction.

Throughout history, people have made bad decisions because they became sexually infatuated or besotted with some fantasy figure. And, as they say, love is blind. More accurately, lust is blind. Some of the greatest music and literature ever created has been about tortured relationships that were built around sex, obsession, betrayal, deception… and illusion.

As I said before, whether you're male or female, your relationship with cigarettes is almost identical to a sexual affair such as this. We've already looked at some of the usual characteristics of affairs. Most affairs start with a rash or impulsive decision, the desire for some romance, excitement, or a quick sexual 'thrill'. The problem is that, just like smoking, the decision to start an affair is usually a lot easier than the decision to end it.

Which brings me to an important point. Never in your life have you made a decision to become (or remain) a lifelong smoker. Why not? Because *your survival instincts would have made it impossible.* Let me explain why. Your brain can easily be reassured by the fact that the next cigarette probably won't kill you, but *it can't be fooled into thinking that smoking won't kill you eventually.* Even if you were suicidal, you'd choose an easier, less ridiculous method to kill yourself.

When you buy a carton of duty frees, do you really relish the idea of smoking hundreds of cigarettes? You've probably never even thought about it like this, have you? But do you really look forward to all that smoke, all that coughing, all that inconvenience, all that wasted money?

Do you really want to smoke all those cigarettes?

No. The only cigarette you can ever look forward to is the next one.

Sexual affairs work the same way. They need to survive on a day-by-day basis, simply because the long-term consequences aren't exactly much of an aphrodisiac, are they? The thought of one more passionate session is always exciting and pleasurable, but how exciting is the prospect of

> YOUR BRAIN CAN easily be reassured by the fact that the next cigarette probably won't kill you, but it can't be fooled into thinking that smoking won't kill you eventually.

keeping the lies and hassle going for the next twenty years?

One of the attendees to an early nicotine trick workshop told me she smoked because she had a 'self-destructive streak'. I asked her why she had chosen such a humiliating and convoluted way of doing herself in. Of course, it soon emerged that *her feeling of desperation had given her this self-destructive streak*. It wasn't there before. She is now a non-smoker and, as far as I'm aware, is no longer considering moving nearer to Beachy Head.

So, if you never took a decision to become a lifelong smoker, what decision did you take?

You took a decision to flirt with smoking, *to see what it felt like, to see how it would make you feel*. If you're like me, you wanted to appear adult and sophisticated, or maybe you were curious, or maybe you felt tempted by the idea of 'being naughty'. Or, like the grieving man I mentioned earlier, maybe you thought smoking would comfort you at a stressful time.

But, however it started, one day you found you were in too deep and couldn't stop. So you were forced to 'retrospectively' make the decision to become a smoker. You were forced to justify your carelessness by inventing a plausible explanation to put you back in control, *a cover story*, or more probably an entire string of them.

In later chapters, I'll discuss all the usual cover stories, and you can quietly cringe as you recognise amongst them your 'personal' reason for smoking, a secret that will just happen to be shared by about a hundred million smokers (all who believe they thought of it first). But don't worry. By the time you start reading these cover stories, you'll already know how the nicotine trick works, which means *you'll be too excited to care about any embarrassment you may feel.*

Every time I present a workshop, I meet someone who claims to be ecstatically happy as a smoker, and who loudly insists that they don't need help of any sort. Sometimes it's someone who's given a lift to someone else who does want to stop. I love talking to these people, because I know what's going to happen and it's absolutely fascinating watching it unfold. Here's what I do. I avoid talking about smoking, because I know I don't even need to bring the subject up. I'll talk about football, or *EastEnders*, or something else. Eventually, I'll create a pause.

And then it happens.

Bang on cue, they 'casually' ask me how I help people to stop smoking. I tell them I wouldn't want to bore them with it, and then I change the subject. This inflames them even further and, soon afterwards, they become frustrated and start suggesting possibilities to me. Despite the fact that I take the nicotine trick very seriously, I sometimes allow myself to be silently amused as the conversation unfolds:

'I suppose you think I'm too weak to quit?'

'Not at all. Actually, you're a lot stronger than me.'

'Stronger?' Their eyes narrow to slits, suspecting a trap. (It is a trap, but not one set by me.)

'Well, you've managed to maintain an illusion for yourself that I wasn't able to maintain. That takes a massive amount of energy, strength and determination'.

This has a similar effect to spraying smoke on bees. They become quiet and subdued for a few moments. There is sometimes a long pause before the next question, but it always arrives eventually.

'What illusion?'

'Oh, haven't you heard? Smokers smoke because of a chemical coincidence that makes them misunderstand the delayed effects of nicotine. It's not rocket science, really. But it does play absolute havoc with them.'

After that, I just can't do it to them any more. I sit down and explain the nicotine trick to them in detail. I tell them how desperately I struggled to stop smoking, and how weak I consider myself to be, but how my cravings simply wore off when I suddenly discovered how nicotine had tricked my brain. As soon as they realise that I don't see myself as the new Messiah and that I have absolutely no desire to 'cure' the planet of smoking, they pour their hearts out to me about how they've lied to themselves and everyone else about why they really smoke. In some cases, they've bottled up an incredible amount of fear, simply because they feel so trapped.

Let's move on. If your relationship with cigarettes is an affair, there must be *a focal point*, some specific driving reason that makes you keep doing it.

There is.

Let's talk about sex.

The Nicotine Orgasm

If you're like most smokers, you probably already have strong views about why you smoke. This is natural. Smokers need strong views. Smoking is such a suicidal thing to do that not having strong views would drive smokers insane.

Some smokers tell me they can stop whenever they want, and I believe them. Even without this book, stopping smoking is easy. Then again, jumping in the air is easy.

Staying there isn't.

You probably know people who've stopped smoking, but how many of them can say for sure that they'll never want to smoke again? Anyone can stop smoking. But very few people stop smoking without ever craving cigarettes again. Let's have a look at why you think you enjoy smoking. But, before we talk about cigarettes, let's talk about pleasure.

> AS ANY DOCTOR will tell you, your body has never experienced pleasure, and it never will. Only your brain can experience pleasure.

As any doctor will tell you, your body has never experienced pleasure, and it never will. *Only your brain can experience pleasure*. Your body simply sends chemical and electrical signals through your nervous system to your brain. And, until these are interpreted, they don't actually mean anything.

In fact, sometimes *exactly the same physical sensation can mean two completely opposite things*. Take an example. If you kiss someone you find sexually attractive, it's extremely pleasurable, isn't it? Not just emotionally, but *physically pleasurable*. But if you were to kiss someone you found repulsive, it would be physically unpleasant.

But wait a second.

In both cases, *the actual physical sensation itself would be identical*. So what's the difference?

The difference is *the context*. It's pleasure by association. Because you *associate* sexual attraction with pleasure, part of your brain decides in advance to *make you enjoy it*. This response is automatic. You don't have any direct control over it.

Just like you don't have any direct control over wanting a cigarette.

Right at the beginning of this book, I told you that you can't simply decide not to love someone. I told you it simply doesn't work like that. It's time for you to understand why. Let's take a look under the bonnet.

You may or may not know that your brain is made up loosely of two halves, the left and right sides. They both do different things. The left side of your brain controls *cognitive and conscious thought*. When you're trying to figure out how long it will be until you can next have a smoking break, or how many duty frees you can afford, you're using the left side of your brain to think, make decisions and so on. While you're awake, this part of you is active and dominant. Imagine a physical computer reacting to deliberate key presses. The left side of your brain is like this. When you go to sleep, so does this part of you.

Then we have the right side of the brain. Your instinctive, emotional, and sexual reactions are based here. When you're attracted to someone, it's the right side of your brain that is controlling this impulse. If you have a phobia or any other 'hang-ups' that seem to defy rational explanation, it's important to realise that these are based, not in your *conscious* mind, but in your *subconscious* mind. This is precisely why the 'pull-yourself-together' approach doesn't work with someone who has a phobia, even when they know the fear is irrational. If you've ever had a phobia, you

LATER, I'M GOING to switch the light on and we'll have a look at it together. What you see will amaze you.

74

already know this is true. Your fear of stopping smoking lives down here, in the dark, with all your other fears. Later, I'm going to switch the light on and we'll have a look at it together. What you see will amaze you.

Your subconscious mind is part of what's known technically as your *autonomic nervous system*. In addition to controlling your emotions and instincts, this part of your brain monitors thousands of vital signs continually, such as your blood pressure, heart rate, temperature, hormone levels, your level of sexual arousal, and so on. It's this part of you that responds automatically to stress or fear by producing adrenalin, which raises your blood pressure and makes you physically tense and ready for action. And, if your subconscious mind tells you to do something...

... it's doing it for a reason.

Psychologists often call these reasons triggers. Usually, these triggers act in your favour, such as eating because you're hungry or sitting near a fire if you're cold. But occasionally, amongst all the millions of 'good' triggers that find their way into your subconscious mind, a 'bad' one gets in there by mistake. This can happen if you're traumatised... and it can happen if you're tricked.

To make sure you understand how this works, let's take a look at the best-known type of 'bad' trigger. Phobias.

THE PHOBIC TRIGGER

Imagine this. A little girl gets bitten on the face by a puppy, which didn't mean to hurt her but was simply overexcited. The child panics, becoming terrified and agitated. At that exact instant, a *phobic trigger* is automatically created in her subconscious mind, a trigger linking dogs with pain and danger.

She now has a phobia of dogs.

That's all it took. A single moment of terror and she is now continually scared of dogs. Of course, her subconscious mind doesn't see this as a 'phobia'. *It sees it as a perfectly logical reaction based on the traumatic experience.* And this reaction is now 'hard-wired' into her brain, always there in the background, waiting to 'protect' her from dogs – *whether she likes it or not.*

Now imagine this. The little girl grows up to become a highly successful businesswoman who is fully able to deal with a room full of clients or colleagues, a woman who is strong, intelligent, determined and… *still terrified of dogs. She still panics when a dog comes near her, even though she thinks that this doesn't 'make sense'.*

This is what a phobia is. It's a subconscious trigger that was created for all the right reasons, *but which is no longer appropriate or helpful.*

Unfortunately, there's a problem. Because the trigger only exists in the woman's *subconscious* mind, it makes absolutely no difference that she *consciously* knows it is no longer appropriate or helpful. Even if the phobia embarrasses her, her panic reaction to dogs is exactly the same every time she sees one. It happens whether she wants it to happen or not.

THIS IS WHAT a phobia is. It's a subconscious trigger that was created for all the right reasons, but which is no longer appropriate or helpful.

The reason for this is amazingly simple. It's because even though she only ever had one painful experience of a dog, the human subconscious mind always decides how to react to a potential threat based on *the most terrifying memory it can find.* When you consider that its sole function is to keep you alive, this makes perfect sense. It needs to react instantly. It doesn't have time to sit down and plough through every related memory it can find, so it simply assumes the 'worst case scenario'.

Let me stress this point once again. It makes no difference how 'illogical' a phobia seems to be. The subconscious mind isn't 'logical', it's automatic and instinctive. It needs to be in order to react immediately to potential threats.

And this is why the woman can't simply 'let go' of the phobia, because this trigger mechanism is *a life-or-death response.* Her subconscious mind can't just ignore this trigger, because *its sole purpose is to protect her.*

Think about it this way. Would you want your subconscious mind to suddenly 'forget' that fire is dangerous, or that driving your car at high speed into a wall is dangerous… *or that smoking a cigarette somehow makes you feel more 'secure'?*

Are you beginning to 'get it'?

Before we start talking about cigarettes, there's one more thing you need to know about your subconscious mind. *In certain situations, it doesn't know the difference between a genuine memory and one you've imagined.* This is why a nightmare can terrify you as much as the real thing. Have you ever had a bad dream about something that would have made you laugh if you'd been awake? Of course you have. We all have. But, at the moment you woke up, your physical reaction was *exactly the same as one produced by genuine danger or threat*. Maybe you were sweating or shaking. Maybe you even cried out in your sleep.

Why have I mentioned this? Because, in the final chapter of this book, I'll teach you a technique that will create a completely new 'memory' of smoking, one that *your subconscious mind will treat as a real memory, one that will permanently change how cigarettes 'feel' to you.*

Okay. It's taken me almost half of this book to make sure you understand how – and why – your brain reacts to certain things. But I promise you that not one word of this information has been wasted.

Now, let's talk about cigarettes.

WHAT HAPPENS WHEN YOU SMOKE

As you probably know, cigarette smoke contains a complicated cocktail of chemicals that includes carbon monoxide, formaldehyde, nicotine, ammonia and benzene, *all lethal poisons*. If you tried to get away with dumping these chemicals at your local waste tip, you'd be arrested, fined and possibly even end up in prison.

And yet, as a smoker, not only are you prepared to *breathe* these chemicals into your lungs, but you're even prepared to *pay* for the privilege.

Why?

It's because, each time you inhale cigarette smoke, your subconscious mind has been tricked into completely misunderstanding what's really happening. Let me explain why.

When I first started trawling through all the scientific information about nicotine and smoking, almost immediately I made a surprising discovery, and it's this. Numerous scientific reports have noted that laboratory animals such as monkeys and dogs will only breathe cigarette smoke if they're absolutely forced to. And, even when they've been forced to smoke thousands of cigarettes, *they'll stop as soon as they physically can* and do everything they can to avoid breathing cigarette smoke ever again. In other words, *they're incapable of getting physical pleasure from smoking*.

The reason this surprised me so much is that, for many years, I was absolutely, totally convinced that cigarettes were giving me some kind of genuine pleasure and relaxation. But I was wrong.

So let me explain to you, once and for all, what really happens when you smoke a cigarette.

When cigarette smoke enters your lungs, two things happen. Firstly, the *carbon monoxide* replaces oxygen in your bloodstream, and makes you feel slightly dizzy and light-headed. Your heart starts beating faster, to replace the missing oxygen, and your blood pressure rises. You're suffering from

> IN THE FINAL chapter of this book, I'll teach you a technique that will create a completely new 'memory' of smoking, one that your subconscious mind will treat as a real memory, one that will permanently change how cigarettes 'feel' to you.

temporary *oxygen starvation*. As a result, your central nervous system goes into a mild spasm, which you can feel all over. In fact, if you think of smoking as a sexual affair, *this sensation is effectively the orgasm – it's the point of maximum intimacy between you and a cigarette.*

Unfortunately, you've been cheated. You got the build-up, you got the heavy breathing, you even got a feeling of 'calming down' afterwards. But there was one thing you didn't get: pleasure.

This might confuse you. Surely you do get physical pleasure from smoking? In fact, you don't get any such thing. To understand why, you need to finally learn the biggest secret about smoking – the nicotine trick.

Part Two –
Withdrawal

The Nicotine Trick –
Smoking's greatest secret
finally revealed

You may wonder why I've started a completely new section in this book in order to continue the explanation of what happens when you smoke. The reason for this is that *smoking has, quite literally, nothing to do with physical pleasure*, as you're about to see.

TO FIND THE answer, we need to go all the way back to the moment your affair with cigarettes started.

As any major scientific report will confirm, even in tiny doses nicotine is a powerful stimulant. But if this is true, why do so many smokers believe the exact opposite, that smoking relaxes them? To find the answer, we need to go all the way back to the moment your affair with cigarettes started.

About an hour after you smoked your first-ever cigarette, your body started to feel a growing sensation of *physical tension* caused by *the delayed effects of nicotine on your nervous system*. This reaction caused your chest to tighten slightly, as well as your face muscles and the diaphragm between your chest and stomach. You know this sensation by another name: withdrawal symptoms.

I've heard people describe this sensation as being similar to an 'itch' or 'physical aggravation' or even 'hunger', but it's actually much more specific than that. When your body first experienced this sensation, your subconscious mind did exactly what it's always done. It matched it against all the memories of when you had the same physical sensation in the past. It immediately found a perfect match…

… *fear*.

You might be surprised by this. Most smokers don't remember feeling consciously frightened after their first cigarette. But don't forget that *fear ranges from mild anxiety all the way up to blind panic*. So let me be absolutely specific about what you felt.

Remember our woman with the dog phobia? You felt exactly as she would if she saw a dog two hundred yards in the distance. It wouldn't be close enough to cause an immediate panic attack, but it would be just enough to make her feel uneasy and anxious.

That's how your subconscious mind started to feel after your first cigarette. Uneasy and anxious.

Here's what happened next. Your subconscious mind couldn't figure out *why* you felt anxious or uneasy, *because it couldn't see any obvious threat*. So it simply sat there feeling slightly uncomfortable and worried.

Now let me tell you something you probably don't know. Around the same time that you started smoking, millions of other people also smoked a single cigarette and have *never been tempted to smoke again ever since*.

Here's why. They smoked one cigarette, realised that it made them feel uneasy and physically tense, and simply didn't want another. About four days afterwards, this 'background' feeling of tension completely faded away *without them even consciously noticing it*, and their subconscious minds were completely calm again.

The overwhelming majority of these people will never have the slightest urge to smoke again, because their subconscious minds now have a *perfect memory* of what the cigarette 'did' – it made them feel anxious and uncomfortable, starting about an hour after smoking it. Their subconscious minds also realise that there is nothing whatsoever to be gained by smoking another cigarette, because they got *absolutely no pleasure from the one they smoked*. They diced with death and got lucky. Nothing more.

But you weren't so lucky. Let me explain why.

You decided to give smoking *another chance* and smoked a second cigarette, which, predictably enough, started the entire process all over again, beginning with a mild feeling of tension. But, because this feeling had been steadily growing stronger ever since you finished the first cigarette, setting the whole process back to the 'beginning' made it feel as though the second cigarette had *relieved this sensation of tension*.

In actual fact, it didn't do any such thing. It

simply started this sensation building up all over again. But, because your body's reaction to nicotine begins with *only a very low level of tension, it felt like smoking the second cigarette had made you feel relaxed*. And, because this feeling of chemical tension had sneaked up on you so gradually in the first place, your mind was already starting to forget that this sensation didn't even exist before you smoked the first cigarette.

Imagine your body's reaction to nicotine as a feeling of mild physical tension that slowly rises in a curve, reaches a peak and then gradually falls away (which is precisely what it does). Just before you lit your second cigarette, *you were on your way up this curve without consciously being aware of it*. By smoking your second cigarette, you effectively pressed a 'restart' button that sent you back to the beginning of the curve. But because you were already part of the way up the curve caused by the first cigarette, going back to the beginning automatically meant you were suddenly feeling

> JUST BEFORE YOU lit your second cigarette, you were on your way up this curve without consciously being aware of it.

a lower level of tension as a direct result of smoking a cigarette.

What you didn't know was that smoking the second cigarette simply started this climb all over again. If you had left it alone, you would have reached the top of the curve after a few hours and the feeling of tension would have simply died away after about four days (as millions of other people have discovered after smoking a single cigarette). But by smoking your second cigarette, you simply delayed the inevitable, and that's all you've done with every cigarette you've smoked ever since.

The simple truth is, once your body's reaction to nicotine starts, other than death there is no way of 'fast-forwarding' to the end of it. Your body doesn't work like that. Of course, you can easily jump back to *the beginning* (by smoking) or you can simply let it run its natural course (by not smoking), but you can never jump past the 'middle bit'. But you've never known this, and this lack of knowledge is why you've been pressing the 'restart' button ever since, causing the feeling of tension to restart again at a lower, *less frightening* level.

Unfortunately, it gets worse. Because *the feeling*

of tension caused by nicotine feels absolutely identical to the feeling of tension caused by genuine fear, from the moment you smoked your second cigarette onwards, your subconscious mind made another serious mistake – it started telling you to smoke, not just when you were experiencing the fake 'chemical fear' caused by the delayed effects of nicotine, but...

... *whenever you really were genuinely scared or stressed!*

This is why, in an office full of people, *even a mild crisis will cause every smoker to want to light up in unison*. This is also why every airport contains bars full of chain-smokers. This is why people chain-smoke outside hospitals, at funerals, in betting shops and *everywhere people are likely to be stressed*. It has nothing to do with getting pleasure or being 'cool' or 'sociable'.

The subconscious minds of every one of those people have been tricked by the chemical properties of nicotine, tricked into believing that smoking a cigarette calms genuine stress, simply because it 'resets' *something that feels similar* (the tension caused by the nicotine in the previous cigarette).

But smoking doesn't reduce *genuine* stress in

the slightest, which is why smokers are always forced to chain-smoke when they're scared or stressed, wondering why each cigarette is somehow failing to 'kick in'.

They're trapped inside a nightmare caused by nothing more than the bizarre chemical properties of nicotine.

But it gets worse still. Because your brain has gradually developed a tolerance to nicotine, every cigarette you now smoke is having less and less effect on the tension caused by the previous cigarette, so your subconscious mind has been getting more anxious and stressed each time you've smoked.

In fact, even if you only smoked a cigarette thirty seconds ago, your body is already starting to become stressed from nicotine. However, you're now so used to feeling like this that you think you feel 'normal'. But you'll only feel 'normal' again when your body is completely free of nicotine.

Let me tell you something. If you smoke cigarettes, every single morning of your life you wake up with a feeling of mild tension in your face, shoulders, stomach and chest. That feeling has become so familiar to you that *it now feels normal*. But, if you were to look into a mirror before smoking your first cigarette of the day, you'd see fear and anxiety in your eyes. This fear is caused by the fact that your body feels 'chemically frightened' by nicotine and your subconscious mind wants you to make it go away – as soon as possible.

> ASK YOURSELF THIS. Did you feel anxious twenty times each day before you started smoking?

Ask yourself this. Did you feel anxious twenty times each day before you started smoking? Did you feel anxious during visits to the pub, or at weddings, or playing pool, or watching television? Did you feel anxious after sex? Did you feel anxious after a nice meal, or with a glass of wine?

Of course you didn't. And that's why you need to keep telling yourself (and everyone else) that you enjoy smoking. Because the alternative is to accept an unspeakable, horrific thought: that your subconscious mind is now anxious even during the best moments of your life.

The depressing truth is that your subconscious mind has been increasingly anxious ever since the moment you started your doomed affair with cigarettes. There's been a shadow over you the entire time, even while you've been asleep.

You've simply got so used to the continual background feeling of chemically induced anxiety that, to keep your sanity, you've been forced to keep telling yourself that cigarettes must *somehow* be pleasurable.

Now ask yourself another question. How many times have you blamed the feeling of tension known as 'withdrawal symptoms' on smoking, rather than on not being able to smoke? Probably never. Like every smoker, your brain somehow sees this sensation as being a consequence of *not smoking*, rather than what it really is: a delayed reaction to the nicotine in the last cigarette you smoked.

Why do you think you've never made this connection?

The answer is the timing.

When you smoke a cigarette, it takes only a few seconds for the nicotine to 'reset' the physical tension to a lower level, but it takes *an hour or so* for this tension to build up all over again. The fact that this feeling of chemically induced tension is a *delayed reaction* means that your subconscious mind – quite understandably – fails to see it as the direct result of smoking a cigarette. Even the phrase 'withdrawal symptoms' suggests that you suffer not as a result of smoking, but as a result of not being able to smoke. You automatically assume you feel this way because you've not smoked the next cigarette yet, but you've got it the wrong way round. *You feel this way because you did smoke the previous cigarette and you're now feeling the delayed effect of it.*

Have you ever had toothache, and deliberately pushed the tooth with your finger so that it hurt twice as much, just so that you could release it and relieve the pain slightly? Children sometimes do this instinctively. The point is, when you stop pushing, the pain is no better than it was to start with, *but it's better than it was when you were pushing,* so it almost feels like genuine pleasure when you take the pressure off.

BECAUSE A CIGARETTE briefly reduces the existing feeling of tension caused by nicotine before causing it all over again, your brain sees a wrong picture of what's happening and is, quite simply, tricked into reaching the wrong conclusion.

This is exactly what happens when you smoke, but with fake chemical 'anxiety' rather than actual pain. You're directly inflicting the sensation known as 'nicotine withdrawal symptoms' on yourself, but *because it's a delayed reaction*, it somehow doesn't 'feel like that', does it? In fact, because a cigarette briefly *reduces* the existing feeling of tension caused by nicotine before causing it all over again, your brain sees a wrong picture of what's happening and is, quite simply, tricked into reaching *the wrong conclusion*.

It's called the nicotine trick.

UNDERSTANDING WITHDRAWAL SYMPTOMS

The widespread perception that 'withdrawal symptoms' are somehow the result of depriving your body of something it 'wants', is a fatal misunderstanding of what nicotine really does. It suggests that nicotine is almost a *beneficial* substance, rather than what it actually is – *a lethal poison that causes a delayed stress reaction when taken in tiny doses and almost certain death when taken in larger doses*.

So why don't most smokers see 'withdrawal symptoms' as the result of smoking a cigarette? Why does this sensation always seem to be viewed as something you get when you stop smoking, but at no other time? After all, wouldn't you agree that the effects of any drug include *everything which happens from the moment the drug is taken until the point where the person is back to the state they were in before they took the drug?* Surely you can't just concentrate on what happens in the first five minutes and then pretend that what happens an hour later is being caused by some unknown, mysterious force from outer space.

But this is exactly what smokers are tricked into doing with 'withdrawal symptoms', and this is why the first thing you need to do is to acknowledge what smoking a cigarette does:

- **Smoking a cigarette directly causes a delayed sensation of physical tension.**

- **Your last cigarette directly caused a delayed sensation of physical tension.**

- **Your next cigarette will directly cause a delayed sensation of physical tension.**

- **The cigarette after that will directly cause a delayed sensation of physical tension.**

- **The last cigarette you ever smoke in**

your life will directly cause a delayed
sensation of physical tension (unless
you die within an hour of smoking it).

• The first cigarette you ever smoked in
your life directly caused a delayed
sensation of physical tension.

• Every cigarette smoked by every
smoker you've ever met in your life
has directly caused a delayed sensation
of physical tension.

• Every cigarette smoked by every
smoker ever to exist on the face of this
planet has directly caused a delayed
sensation of physical tension.

• Every cigarette which will ever be
smoked in the future by every smoker
who will ever exist on the face of this
planet will directly cause a delayed
sensation of physical tension.

You can't blame a hangover on not drinking. It's
caused by drinking. You can't blame indigestion

on not eating. It's caused by eating. You can't blame 'withdrawal symptoms' on not being able to smoke.

They're caused by smoking.

And yet the effects of smoking are often presented to smokers in such an incredibly twisted way that

SMOKING A CIGARETTE directly causes a delayed sensation of physical tension.

millions of people have been prevented from seeing the real picture. In fact, a more accurate name for *nicotine withdrawal symptoms* would be, quite simply, *delayed nicotine symptoms*. Think about it. You can't possibly get this feeling of chemical tension by not smoking *unless you've recently smoked*. Where else do you think these so-called 'symptoms' come from? The Moon? Neptune? The Twilight Zone?

No. They come from smoking. If a non-smoker decides that he's never going to smoke a cigarette, does he immediately get 'withdrawal symptoms' as a result of the decision not to smoke? Does his chest tighten? Do his face muscles become tense?

Of course not. You can't get this feeling by not smoking.

You get it by smoking.

This also means that the only way to get what your subconscious mind really wants (the end of the fake stress caused by nicotine) *is to not smoke*. That way, it's gone in a few days. All you need to do is make your subconscious mind see this.

But isn't this difficult? Surely your subconscious mind does what it wants. How do you know it's even listening? Well, we'll talk about that in a few seconds. But first, it's time for you to make a decision. It may be unexpected, but you're ready.

Here it is.

You are never going to smoke another cigarette in your life. From this second onwards, you are already a non-smoker.

Let me repeat that.

You are never going to smoke another cigarette in your life. From this second onwards, you are already a non-smoker.

I'm lying. Smoke whenever you want.

I just made you feel anxious and uncomfortable, didn't I? I just made some hidden part of you fight against what I was telling you, even though you think you want to 'stop smoking'.

That part of you is your subconscious mind, and

it's been listening to everything I've been saying. It just reacted the way it did because it perceived my statement as *a direct threat to you*. It's trying to protect you from me because it's still in the grip of the nicotine trick. The truth is, at this second in your life, *your subconscious mind still doesn't want you to stop smoking and I've just proved it*.

I've also demonstrated the real reason why you're so convinced it's difficult to stop smoking. Because your subconscious mind keeps reacting exactly like it just did a few seconds ago.

But what if you could find a way to stop it doing this? Would you still have cravings to smoke?

YOU WILL NEVER, ever find the cigarette that will permanently satisfy you, because it's cigarettes that are causing you to feel stressed.

The answer is no. In fact, if you can somehow find a way to stop your subconscious mind reacting in this way, you'll be removing the only barrier to instantly becoming a non-smoker.

And I'm going to show you exactly how to do it.

The subconscious belief that smoking is the solution to anxiety (rather than the cause of it) is the twisted deception known as the nicotine trick. But a trick is still a trick, and an illusion is still an illusion. And this is why the last cigarette you smoked didn't satisfy you, this is why the next cigarette will always be followed by the one afterwards. You will never, ever find the cigarette that will permanently satisfy you, because it's cigarettes that are causing you to feel stressed.

MASTERS OF MANIPULATION

If you still feel that cigarettes are pleasurable, consider this. The cigarette industry spends billions of dollars promoting smoking as being enjoyable and sociable. Not millions of dollars… *billions*!

Why? Think about it for a second. If cigarettes really were capable of giving pleasure, why would the tobacco giants need to spend such astronomical sums of money on making your subconscious mind *associate* cigarettes with pleasure?

Of course, the official story is that the cigarette companies are simply competing for 'market share', but actually this doesn't stand up when illuminated by the facts. There are only a handful of tobacco giants, there's very little genuine competition in the global cigarette market. These guys could save billions and billions of dollars by simply letting people decide whether they want to smoke or not. So, let me ask the question again:

Why spend so much?

They're spending this money, not just to lure millions of new young smokers into the grasp of the nicotine trick, but also to keep existing smokers like you permanently distracted from their real reason for smoking. They want to make sure you die without ever understanding that the real reason you smoked all those cigarettes wasn't pleasure at all.

It was fear.

Let me embarrass you briefly in order to make a further point. The first time you ever had a real orgasm, it was pleasurable, wasn't it? You didn't need to learn how to enjoy it because the pleasure is *real* and *physical*. So, if cigarettes also provide pleasure, why wasn't your first cigarette pleasurable?

> IF CIGARETTES REALLY were capable of giving pleasure, why would the tobacco giants need to spend such astronomical sums of money on making your subconscious mind associate cigarettes with pleasure?

Do you see what I'm getting at? Even using the most basic logic, it's easy to prove beyond all doubt that smoking isn't driven by pleasure.

Let me put it to you another way. When you feel sexually turned-on, it's enjoyable and exciting, but *only because you know that satisfying it will be pleasurable.* But what if you were promised fantastic sex, and then forced instead to take a freezing cold shower in dirty water? And what if this humiliation was forced on you twenty times every single day for the rest of your life, *and* you had to pay a fortune for it, *and* it was going to ruin your skin, hair and teeth, *and* it was going to cause your arteries to harden, *and* it was going to give you lung cancer and *you were never going to get a single moment of pleasure from it?*

THE NET RESULT of smoking a cigarette is less than zero. What's the point of reducing physical tension for a few minutes if the only result is to create several more days of identical physical tension?

It would drive you absolutely insane with frustration, wouldn't it?

But don't you see – *that's the situation you are in.* And that's why you're so miserable and confused, because you keep wanting to smoke, even though deep inside you know that cigarettes, quite simply, *don't work*. The net result of smoking a cigarette is less than zero. What's the point of reducing physical tension for a few minutes if the only result is to create several more days of identical physical tension? It's like paying a hundred pounds for a five pound note. It's like a lifetime of teasing foreplay followed by cold showers.

It's an embarrassing, pathetic, demeaning, futile, waste of your life.

Be honest. When it comes to your affair with cigarettes, who's screwing who?

Even when people stop smoking (or more accurately, *try* to stop smoking), most keep desperately chasing the impossible dream and crawling back to their cigarettes again and again and again, due to some invisible force which they don't understand. In sexual terms, this is exactly the same as repeatedly ending a disappointing relationship, only to go back to it 'just for the sex', only to then realise that *the lousy sex was why you finished it in the first place*. You never really finished it at all. All you ever did was throw a tantrum because you felt scared, frustrated and let down. But by going back, you've forced yourself to end it all over again. And while you're wasting all this time, you could be finding real pleasure somewhere else.

Anywhere else.

Are you beginning to see why your reason for smoking has been so agonisingly difficult to explain until now? Are you also beginning to see why billions of dollars are spent on brainwashing smokers into associating cigarettes with pleasure? Unfortunately, it's an illusion that you've been forced to go along with, because you've had no real alternative. Until now.

WHY SMOKING IS A PLEASURE-FREE ZONE

At this point, there may be some stubborn part of your mind still clinging to the idea that your body really does enjoy cigarettes. If so, I've got a confession to make.

I envy you.

The moment that I finally knew for sure that smoking cannot provide physical pleasure was one of the most amazing moments of my entire life, because that was the moment that the fear and uncertainty finally disappeared.

Even without going into all the scientific data about the extremely unpleasant effects of cigarette smoke, let me use a simple piece of logic to prove, one more time, that *you cannot possibly smoke for pleasure*.

Right now, I want you to think of one of your favourite pieces of music, and imagine it playing. Now, you obviously get a lot of pleasure and enjoyment from listening to this song, otherwise, it wouldn't be one of your favourites, would it? But let me ask you three simple 'yes or no' questions about the pleasure of listening to your favourite song:

- **If you were told that you couldn't listen to this song for a few days, would it cause you to panic or to become anxious?**

- **Have you ever felt a desperate need to listen to this song when you were stressed, or immediately before a long flight?**

- **Would you stand outside in a howling gale looking like an idiot for no other**

reason than to listen to this song on your Walkman?

No, no and no. Because these actions – familiar to all smokers – aren't based on *pleasure*. They're based on *fear*. And this means that the only thing that matters when it comes to escaping from cigarettes is *removing the fear*.

Which brings me to the central conclusion of this book, a conclusion that goes against almost all the established 'wisdom' on nicotine and smoking. It's a conclusion that the cigarette industry quietly reached decades ago and which drives much of their advertising and packaging. It's also a conclusion most smokers instinctively know is true as soon as they hear it. The conclusion is this. Even though most people insist that smoking is either habit or addiction, it isn't. In fact your affair with cigarettes is really driven by nothing less than a mild, chemically induced phobia, a phobia which exists because nicotine

WHICH BRINGS ME to the central conclusion of this book, a conclusion that goes against almost all the established 'wisdom' on nicotine and smoking.

withdrawal symtoms feel identical to genuine fear.

Let me explain this a little further.

Most physically addictive drugs are considered to be addictive because they provide two things – a feeling of *intense physical pleasure* or *well-being* when they're taken, and *terrible withdrawal symptoms* when the addict tries to stop. *But smoking actually does neither* and yet some mysterious force still makes it impossible to give up.

That mysterious force is the phobia triggered by the fake chemical 'anxiety' that is created by smoking a cigarette, and the infuriating time delay that causes your brain to overlook the fact that smoking a cigarette was the direct cause of it.

Smoking is a phobia. It's a phobia caused by your body's delayed reaction to nicotine and the fact that it feels identical to genuine fear, which – unbeknown to your conscious mind – triggers a panic reaction, telling you to… smoke a cigarette!

Here's a statistic that might interest you. Did you know that smokers who describe themselves as 'nicotine addicts' actually suffer *worse withdrawal symptoms* when they try to stop than those who consider smoking to be merely a 'habit'?

This is because the belief in chronic physical addiction reinforces the belief that stopping smoking will be physically painful. This, predictably enough, creates massive fear, which the terrified individual then mistakes for physical withdrawal symptoms, which causes even more fear. This is known as a 'phobic reaction', essentially a spiralling panic attack.

YOU KEEP SMOKING to avoid this happening, to keep it under your control. Your phobia is essentially a fear of fear itself.

You keep smoking to avoid this happening, to keep it under your control. Your phobia is essentially a fear of fear itself. And deep inside… you've always known this, haven't you?

Remember again that your body's delayed stress reaction to nicotine doesn't do any real damage, it's *the panic that this sensation causes, the phobic reaction* that keeps driving you to light up. As many other books have correctly pointed out, by itself the feeling of 'nicotine withdrawal symptoms' is an extremely vague sensation and there is no pain whatsoever. What does the damage is *your subconscious mind mistaking this sensation for fear and becoming genuinely terrified, particularly if you can't smoke!*

If you still find it hard to believe that smoking is a phobia rather than an addiction, do what I did. Find any scientific report on smoking, or even look up the phrase 'nicotine withdrawal symptoms' on an internet search engine (try Yahoo!, Lycos, Google, Mamma, any of them). Then compare these 'symptoms' with the symptoms of anxiety. You'll find that they're more than just similar. They're identical!

You'll find them listed as 'nervousness, tremors, irritability, sleeplessness, lack of concentration, loss of appetite' and so on. All of which just happen to be symptoms of severe anxiety, such as that caused by a phobia.

What a coincidence!

But don't just take my word for it. Take another look at what you've suffered in the past when you tried to stop smoking. Was there any bleeding, itching, hair loss, reduced bone mass, impairment of hearing or vision, or any other physical symptoms of any genuine disease you've ever heard of?

No. You were actually suffering nothing more than the effects of fear.

But why?

Because you triggered your phobia by trying to stop smoking.

Now the good news. Once you correct the subconscious misunderstandings that have created this phobia, your subconscious mind will be no more likely to tell you to smoke than it is to make you pour petrol over yourself and set fire to it.

YOU NEED TO make your subconscious mind see that the feeling of sensation caused by smoking doesn't need a panic reaction of any kind.

It's only been telling you to smoke because of the phobia known as the nicotine trick. Beat the nicotine trick, and you've beaten smoking. It's as simple as that.

Don't forget, genuine fear or anxiety is made up of two things. The first is the actual threat itself. The second is *the physical sensation caused by your response to it.* With the delayed reaction caused by nicotine, all you've got is the second part, or more accurately, something that feels like it. There is no actual threat and this means you don't need to 'fight' it at all because *it doesn't actually mean anything.*

If you're like most smokers, maybe you believe that 'withdrawal symptoms' and 'cravings' are actually the same thing. Maybe you believe that whenever you have this underlying feeling of tension, it automatically means you'll want a cigarette. This is totally wrong. Millions of non-smokers who work in smoky environments (such as pubs or bars) breathe in a large amount of nicotine just from the secondary smoke. As a result, they wake up each morning with exactly the same feeling of nicotine-induced tension as smokers do. In most cases, they have absolutely no desire to light up.

Why not? Because *it's not this feeling which causes you to smoke*. It's the false connection which exists in your subconscious brain, the fatal misunderstanding which *translates* this feeling into the desire to smoke. By the time you finish this book, this false connection will no longer exist, so it won't make any difference whether the feeling of tension lasts three days or four days or seven thousand years, or how weak or strong it is, or anything else.

I still eat in restaurants. I still drink in pubs. I regularly encourage smokers to test the nicotine trick in front of me by smoking. Which means I still breathe cigarette smoke, which further means I still sometimes wake up with the feeling of tension caused by nicotine. But my sub-conscious brain now knows precisely what this sensation is (and precisely what caused it), so it never triggers the desire to smoke.

You need to make your subconscious mind see that the feeling of sensation caused by smoking doesn't need a panic reaction of any kind, because it represents exactly the same level of genuine threat that a puppy represents to the woman with the phobia of dogs: none at all!

It's like an alarm that keeps going off by mistake. It's a phobic reaction to the physical sensation caused by your delayed reaction to smoking a cigarette. That's all it is. As soon as your sub-conscious mind has been put straight on this, it will stop panicking and your core reason for smoking will disappear whether you want it to or not!

But the news gets even better. Imagine that the delayed feeling of tension caused by nicotine lasted four months after smoking your last ever cigarette. This would mean that if you were to stop smoking, you'd feel mild physical tension for four months. Would this be a major problem? No, because if you're a smoker, you feel this sensation all the time anyway, and *you're going to have it for the rest of your life if you keep smoking*.

But it would mean that after four months, you'd be permanently free of it and your body would finally be capable of relaxing for the first time since you started smoking.

It would be a nice situation, don't you think?

But get this. The delayed feeling of tension caused by nicotine doesn't take four months to disappear...

... *it takes about four days!*

In fact, just *two days* after a person stops smoking, the sensation of physical tension caused by nicotine drops to about *the same level that it drops to as the immediate result of smoking a cigarette*.

But there's a key difference. When you smoke a cigarette, the feeling of tension drops to this level *and then immediately starts to rise again*. If you don't smoke for two days, it drops to this level and *then keeps falling* until it disappears permanently. This means that, even if 'nicotine withdrawal symptoms' were absolute agony, all you'd need to do is stop smoking for just two days and they'd already have fallen lower than they've ever been *even while you've been physically smoking a cigarette!*

You're almost certainly thinking exactly the same as I was when I first discovered how smoking works. It hardly sounds believable, does it? What about all those times you've tried to stop smoking and were still going through hell weeks later? Surely that was your body crying out for a cigarette, wasn't it?

No it wasn't.

It was your subconscious mind screaming in alarm because it thought you were trying to throw away your own safety net. It thought you were trying to put yourself in danger. Don't forget that it thinks that smoking is a cure for fear and anxiety, and if it thinks that while you smoke, why wouldn't it think that three weeks after you've stopped, or three months, or even three years? A phobia doesn't disappear just because it's not been triggered for a while. As any psychologist will confirm, it only disappears when your subconscious mind *stops seeing danger where it doesn't exist* and relaxes.

SMOKING IS A vicious cycle driven by an irrational fear of the delayed response to nicotine and the way it pretends to be genuine fear.

That's how it works.

Smoking is a phobia, which means you absolutely *cannot* stop smoking without the permission of your own subconscious mind, unless you want to put yourself through hell. What's more, you've always instinctively known this. All I've done is put what you already knew into words and explained the simple facts behind why it happens.

If you force yourself to stop smoking, you'll be doing the equivalent of our woman with the dog phobia forcing herself to walk into Battersea Dogs Home. That's what it will feel like each time you can't smoke. But I don't need to tell you this. You already know it. How many times have you panicked when you thought you didn't have any cigarettes left?

Why?

Pleasure?

No.

Addiction?

No.

Habit?

No.

Smoking is a phobia.

Smoking is a vicious cycle driven by an irrational fear of the delayed response to nicotine and the way it pretends to be genuine fear. It's a scratched record that will jump from panic response to panic response for the rest of your life – unless you do something about it. This fact may seem terrifying, but you should take comfort from it because it actually means you're faced with a very simple task – a task that I'm going to walk you through, step by step, a bit later on.

* * * * *

You can hide your head in the sand for the rest of your life, but the reality of smoking tobacco hasn't changed since the first cigarette was smoked on this planet, and nothing can make this reality change – ever. The reality of smoking is *exactly the same pathetic, panic-stricken mess it always has been and always will be.*

> THE REALITY OF smoking tobacco hasn't changed since the first cigarette was smoked on this planet, and nothing can make this reality change – ever.

Have you ever put your mouth round a car exhaust and tried to breath the fumes straight into your lungs?

Of course not. *That would be stupid, wouldn't it?*

Well, I've got news for you. It would make more sense than smoking. At least it's free. *You really think that buying a box of twenty rolled-up paper tubes containing tobacco, and smoking them one after another makes sense?* It doesn't matter whether you put each cigarette into one of those long 'elegant' holders, or whether you smoke menthol-flavoured cigarettes, or whether you use a solid gold lighter to light them, or whether you stand on your head and sing the national anthem of Venezuela each time you smoke.

You smoke because your subconscious mind has fallen for the phobia known as the nicotine trick. Your body is just the stooge. It's your mind that has smoked all those cigarettes, because it's been anxious and frightened.

Interestingly, nicotine isn't the only drug that can produce *physical sensations that are usually caused by emotions.* Many other drugs do the same thing. In fact, some are developed specifically for this purpose.

Take an example. Viagra, the drug that is used to treat impotence.

Now, we all know what happens to a man physically when he's sexually aroused. But imagine this. Let's say a man *isn't* sexually aroused, but someone gives him a Viagra tablet without him knowing it. A few minutes later, he has the physical symptoms of sexual arousal. What happens inside his head as a result? If you're a man, maybe you're shrugging and pretending you don't know, but I guarantee most women can guess the answer easily enough. Research suggests that, in most cases, *the mind follows the cues sent by the body*. I won't put it any more explicitly than that, except to say that we men don't need much encouragement to start thinking about sex.

NICOTINE 'CREATES' THE physical sensation of anxiety artificially and the mind is then tricked into reacting by making the mood match the sensation.

Can you see where I'm going with this? Smoking plays the same trick, but with *fear* instead of sexual arousal. Nicotine 'creates' the physical sensation of anxiety *artificially* and the mind is then tricked into reacting by making the mood match the sensation. *Fake fear causes real fear because it implies threat and danger.* And, in the first few seconds after the first drag of a cigarette, the temporary (and partial) reduction in the synthetic, chemical component of that 'fear' feels like the relief you'd get as a result of escaping from a dangerous or stressful situation.

Some 'experts' describe the feeling of 'nicotine withdrawal symptoms' as an 'itch', or even a 'hunger' for nicotine, but *this is absolutely wrong*. By definition, an 'itch' is always irritating. By definition, 'hunger' always cries out to be satisfied. The feeling of tension caused by nicotine does neither of these things *unless your brain is in the grip of the nicotine trick*.

As I mentioned earlier, millions of non-smokers experience 'nicotine withdrawal symptoms' throughout their entire lives without even noticing it, let alone having any desire to smoke. What about all the bar staff, restaurant workers, and all those millions of non-smoking wives, husbands, girlfriends, employees? For this multitude of people, the only thing they notice is the irritation of breathing cigarette smoke, and possibly the smell. But how often do you hear these non-smokers tell you that their bodies are craving nicotine, or that they have an 'itch'? Not often. If you think this is because they don't 'get enough nicotine', think again. It takes only a tiny amount of nicotine to cause that feeling of tension.

This may seem like a subtle difference

between this book and many others, but it's a crucial one. Provided you understand what keeps causing this feeling of tension, it represents neither 'an itch' nor 'hunger'. It represents absolutely nothing more than an artificial chemical feeling of tension caused by your body's delayed reaction to nicotine, that's all.

The first time you smoked a cigarette, you developed this feeling but your subconscious mind had no idea that smoking another cigarette would reduce it. It wasn't a physical 'itch' or 'hunger' then, any more than it needs to be now. *By itself, it didn't make you want to 'do' anything, which is why millions of people smoke one cigarette each year without bothering with a second.*

But smoking your second cigarette *gave this sensation a false meaning, a meaning that has left it terrified of letting go of smoking.* And, until you remove this false meaning, your subconscious mind will keep telling you to smoke until the day you die. You can't escape from your phobia without *absorbing the reasons why the fear is irrational.*

You may find it extremely frustrating that your subconscious brain keeps telling you to smoke, but you shouldn't be. Based on the information it has, *it's actually doing exactly the right thing*. Never forget that, in an emergency (or a perceived emergency), your subconscious mind will automatically make you take *the quickest possible route* to safety (or perceived safety). When you smoke a cigarette, it doesn't matter to your subconscious mind that the cigarette will create physical tension in an hour's time, because it will reduce it *now*. It's not a conscious thing, it's automatic, instinctive, *you have no direct control over it*.

* * * * *

Consider this. I've already explained that, if you stop smoking for as little as two days, the feeling of physical tension caused by nicotine will drop to the same level that is 'achieved' by smoking a cigarette. Even better, it will continue to fall, whereas it will start to rise again if you use a cigarette to do the same thing.

But if this is the case, why does your subconscious mind keep telling you to use a method of reducing the tension that will simply cause it all over again? The answer is infuriatingly simple.

Even though smoking a cigarette is the least effective way of getting rid of the feeling of tension, it just happens to be *the quickest*!

Do you think your subconscious mind would ever tell you to throw yourself off a tall building to certain death? Believe it or not, the answer is yes, *if the situation seems desperate enough*. For instance, if your subconscious mind had a choice between letting you burn to death or jump from a great height, it would tell you to take your chances with the fall. Why? The answer is again infuriatingly simple: it's quicker!

EVEN WHEN PEOPLE have had legs amputated through smoking, their subconscious minds will keep telling them to smoke, because the wrong connections that drive their smoking will never, ever just 'disappear' by themselves.

Your subconscious mind will always try to choose the best (or 'least bad' option) for you. *When it tells you to smoke, that's what it thinks it's doing*. It's responding the only way it knows to a completely unnatural sensation that has confused and frightened it. This is why, even when people have had legs amputated through smoking, their subconscious minds will keep telling them to smoke, because the wrong connections that drive their smoking will never, *ever* just 'disappear' by themselves.

It doesn't work like that, remember?

A brand new gleaming 747 jumbo jet will quite happily fly itself into the side of a mountain killing everyone on board *if the auto-pilot has been programmed with incorrect data.* It won't know it's doing that, because it has no intrinsic intelligence of its own, but it will still do it. That's why the auto-pilot on a 747 is checked and double-checked before take-off. But if, as a pilot, *you knew the auto-pilot was set incorrectly* and you still insisted on engaging it, there would be only one word for the catastrophe that would follow:

Suicide.

Don't ever forget that your subconscious mind is exactly like the auto-pilot I've just mentioned. It reacts to feelings, instincts, connections. Its reaction to smoking isn't based on an in-depth evaluation of the scientific facts, any more than our woman's phobia of dogs is based on a genuine assessment of how dangerous dogs are. It's based on how cigarettes 'feel', what they seem to 'do'.

But here's a sobering thought – if you know

for a fact that your internal auto-pilot is doing something wrong… *the responsibility for correcting it is yours.*

Fortunately, the rest of this book has been written with no other function than to make it easy for you to do exactly this. I'm going to talk you through it, step by step.

I'm almost running out of different ways to repeat the central facts of the nicotine trick, but they're so crucially important that they need to be repeated and repeated and repeated, so let me just spell it out for you one more time.

- **You smoke because the delayed feeling of physical tension caused by nicotine reminds your subconscious mind of fear, and because smoking, while causing this sensation all over again, briefly reduces it first. But the sensation is artificial, chemical, synthetic so it doesn't mean anything. It's a chemical reaction, nothing more. It has no strength by itself.**

- **You smoke, not because of what this sensation does, but because of**

what it reminds your subconscious
mind of – fear.

- **Smoking is a phobia, not an addiction or
  a habit. It's an irrational, confused fear
  of the delayed reaction caused by nicotine.**

The truth is, the word 'addiction' doesn't really
mean anything by itself, the term is descriptive
rather than explanatory. Gambling is 'addictive'
to some people, but there's no drug involved.
Smoking is only 'addictive' because of the
phobia known as the nicotine trick.

Another subtle mistake I've read in some books
about smoking is that smoking partially 'relieves'
the nicotine withdrawal symptoms caused by the
previous cigarette. But the word 'relieve' implies
that the feeling of tension caused by nicotine is
painful or distressing in its own right. This isn't
the case. The correct phrase is 'temporarily
reduce', because the sensation by itself means
nothing *unless you give it permission to frighten you.*

Last week, I took a call from a young woman
who attended a recent nicotine trick workshop.
She called to tell me that she actually *enjoyed
feeling physically tense from nicotine for a few days*

after she stopped smoking, she almost wished it hadn't disappeared so quickly because the feeling of suddenly *not being scared by it any more* was so amazing!

This makes perfect sense. How can you possibly be scared of a physical sensation that you've had, to some degree or other, for *every second of your entire smoking life*? In every situation, good or bad, you've had this physical sensation shadowing you, but you've coped with it. Get it straight in your head. Cigarettes have hit you with their best shot, and you've still managed to carry on living your life. It doesn't take willpower to stop smoking once you understand the nicotine trick…

IN ESSENCE, YOUR relationship with cigarettes is simple. It's a sado-masochistic affair, but one where any pleasure is purely a piece of self-deception.

… it takes willpower to *carry on* smoking!

In case you didn't realise it, your cage door is now half open. But, even at this point, you're probably not quite ready to walk through it.

That's fine. I haven't finished yet.

The moment my subconscious mind finally realised that it no longer needed to hold onto the phobia known as the nicotine trick was the moment the key finally turned in the lock. I almost wish I could have that moment all over again, but I can't.

Fortunately, you've still got that moment to look forward to, if you want it. When it happens, it will be absolutely amazing. It will be one of the most enjoyable things that will ever happen to you. Cigarettes will finally lose their power over you forever, the spell will be completely broken.

In essence, your relationship with cigarettes is simple. It's a sado-masochistic affair, but one where any pleasure is purely a piece of self-deception, an illusion that is needed to mask *the fear that really drives it*. And any relationship based on fear is always going to end in tears. There's only ever one question: who's going to end it?

Okay. You now know why you really smoke. But there's something else you need to know. You need to know how you've helped with the cover-up.

The Need for a Cover Story

When I was working in a huge office a few years ago, there was a woman (I'll call her Sarah) who was having a miserable affair with a married man, the office 'Romeo' (although, to keep the Shakespeare theme going, I'll call him King Leer).

Sarah was an extremely intelligent, attractive, independent woman. King Leer, on the other hand, was a selfish, conceited twerp with no feelings for Sarah, his wife, or the myriad other women he was chasing round the office. (If you're male, I'm sorry if I'm letting the side down with this blasphemous anti-male stuff, but you wouldn't have liked this guy either.)

Every time King Leer disappeared with another woman for an extended 'lunch', Sarah insisted that he had 'family problems' that needed 'attending to'. When people pointed out that he'd already betrayed his wife, she insisted this was because his wife had 'treated him badly'.

When people pointed out that this was King Leer's umpteenth affair, she said it was because he was 'insecure'.

When people pointed out that he was openly boasting that she was just one of many, she insisted it was just office gossip and that he 'must have been misquoted'.

In fact, Sarah had carefully prepared cover

stories for every eventuality, so in the end, people finally stopped warning her about King Leer and his testosterone-fuelled rampage.

It all went wrong. But, as soon as Sarah realised what type of individual King Leer really was, the truth flooded in, her fear of losing him disappeared, and *her affair effectively ended by itself*.

Now, years after it happened, what do you think Sarah would make of the cover stories if they were put to her? Would she still insist that they were reasonable? Probably not. The point is, her cover stories weren't reasoned, factual arguments. They were generated *through necessity, through fear and anxiety*. They allowed her to keep hold of an illusion. But without the illusion itself, why would she need them any more?

The answer is she wouldn't. They only ever existed to allow her to maintain a false view of her situation because the real situation would have hurt her too much if she'd accepted it.

Now ask yourself whether you find the following situation hurtful. Ask yourself whether you really want to accept the following summary of yourself as a smoker:

You smoke because your subconscious mind can't tell the difference between the physical tension caused by the delayed effects of nicotine, and the physical tension caused by genuine fear or anxiety. As a result, your subconscious mind keeps panicking and trying to get rid of this sensation by telling you to smoke, which simply reduces it for a few minutes while causing it all over again.

But your subconscious mind doesn't know that smoking causes this sensation because it's a delayed effect. So it's gradually become more and more anxious and told you to smoke more and more cigarettes, which just keeps causing this feeling of tension all over again.

YOU'VE FALLEN FOR the oldest trick in the book, and you may end up dying as a result.

You've fallen for the oldest trick in the book, and you may end up dying as a result.

Be honest. It's hardly ideal, is it?

So, let's have a think. What I'm looking for is a handful of plausible-sounding cover stories to enable you to keep your affair with cigarette going without facing up to the depressing truth about why you really smoke. Give me a moment or two.

Bingo. I've got it. How about these:

- Smoking makes it easier for you to concentrate.

- Smoking makes you more confident.

- Smoking helps you to keep your weight down.

- Smoking is a habit.

Now, before I go any further, I'm fully aware that one or more of these beliefs probably do sound plausible to you. The reason they sound plausible is because, until you fully understand the nicotine trick, *they are plausible*.

When you smoked your second-ever cigarette, the subconscious part of your brain was tricked into thinking that you'd just relieved genuine fear or

> WHEN YOU SMOKED your second-ever cigarette, your subconscious brain was tricked into thinking that you'd just relieved genuine fear or stress.

stress. In fact, all you really did was temporarily reduce a sensation that simply felt like stress or fear while creating this sensation all over again.

But you didn't know this at the time, did you?

If you had known it, you'd have correctly surmised that your subconscious mind was reacting irrationally. After all, what normal, self-respecting person would allow part of their brain to malfunction without *doing something?* It would have been too humiliating. So you needed a reason, one

ONE MAJOR SCIENTIFIC report correctly describes a smoker's first cigarette as a noxious pharmacological experience.

that sounded plausible, one that would allow you to hold your head up high and claim (or rather, admit) to being a smoker without immediately bursting into tears of shame, embarrassment and despair.

I suspect you're feeling a little uncomfortable at this point, and this is only natural. This book isn't easy reading, and I make no apologies for that. But let's lighten it up a bit. Let's play a game.

Role play.

I *want you to pretend, for the next few minutes, that you've never smoked in your life.*

Assume I'm a senior salesman for the cigarette industry and I'm trying to get you to smoke *just two cigarettes.* My sales manager has explained to me that *it's absolutely crucial that I get you to smoke two cigarettes rather than just one.* Here's why. The first cigarette will knock you absolutely sick. It will irritate your central nervous system, your lungs, your stomach and all your internal organs. The radioactive smoke will get in your nose and throat and make you cough, and the combination of poisons and irritants might even cause you to vomit. Your immediate reaction will be one of extreme disgust and disappointment. One major scientific report correctly describes a smoker's first cigarette as a *noxious pharmacological experience.* In other words, smoking a cigarette is not just unpleasant, but *extremely unpleasant*, at least to start with.

But, an hour or so after smoking a cigarette, something very strange and subtle will happen. Your subconscious mind will become aware of a vague physical sensation similar to fear, *even though this will be nothing more than an artificial chemical sensation that simply feels like fear or anxiety.*

As a cigarette salesman, I happen to know something else. If, like hundreds of millions of people, you don't smoke a second cigarette, your subconscious mind will automatically reach exactly the correct conclusion, which is that cigarettes make you feel physically tense and uneasy about an hour after smoking them and *do not give pleasure or relaxation*. You won't need to persuade yourself that this is the case, your subconscious mind will do it for you (whether you like it or not). If this happens, *both your conscious and subconscious minds will be in total agreement. There will be no conflict, no confusion, and therefore…*

… no phobia!

Of course, you'll feel a bit uneasy and physically tense for three or four days *because you smoked a cigarette*, but you'll hardly even notice it and it will be gone before you know it.

As a cigarette salesman, I'm painfully aware of this fact, and *this is precisely why my sales manager has told me I need to make sure you smoke a second cigarette while you're still feeling tense from the effects of the first one. Because otherwise, you'll never fall for the nicotine trick.* Your affair with cigarettes won't start, because the false connection on which it's based won't be established.

And that's no use to me. As a cigarette salesman, I'm not going to make much commission from selling just one cigarette (even at UK prices). *I've only got one single chance to trap you*, and it's based on a secret piece of inside information that has been deliberately hidden from hundreds of millions of smokers. You see, I happen to know that, if I can somehow get you to smoke *a second cigarette*, it will be just as disgusting as the first one, but…

> WELL, WHY DON'T we try something right now? Why don't I try selling you on the idea of smoking these two cigarettes based on some of the cover stories smokers use?

… before the nicotine in this cigarette causes yet more physical tension, *it will briefly reduce the feeling of physical tension caused by the nicotine in the previous cigarette.*

By itself, this will mean absolutely nothing, because this feeling of tension isn't painful in any way, and it won't be fear or anxiety, but it will be a sensation that *your subconscious mind mistakes for fear and anxiety.* And, because your subconscious mind mistakes it for fear and anxiety, it will believe that reducing it by smoking this second cigarette has made you feel less frightened and anxious.

And that's why, if I can somehow find a way to trick you into smoking this second cigarette, I'll be getting you to step into an absolute nightmare, a burning wheel that you'll then be forced to push round and round for the rest of your life without ever moving you forwards an inch, taking away your health, peace of mind and happiness, and making money for me and my faceless corporate bosses with each desperate spin of the wheel.

Now for the really big question. As a cigarette salesmen, how am I going to trick you into smoking these two cigarettes in the first place?

Well, why don't we try something right now? Why don't I try selling you on the idea of smoking these two cigarettes *based on some of the reasons smokers actually give for smoking*? I want you to imagine how they'd sound coming from me in my guise as a cigarette salesman.

So let's set it up. You're the curious non-smoker and I'm the cigarette salesman. You've not yet smoked either of the cigarettes I'm holding out to you. You're not convinced. You've heard some bad stories about cigarettes, you've heard that cigarette smoke contains a chemical called polonium-210, which gives off radiation inside your lungs and causes tumours to start growing and ripping your lungs apart.

I'm extremely alarmed that you know this. My

eyes narrow. My fake smile falters slightly and I blush slightly underneath my equally fake tan, but I manage to recover before you notice.

Then I start my pitch. I tell you that smoking will improve your concentration. Immediately, you say:

'I don't think so. Every smoker I've ever seen is driven to distraction by anxiety and stress. How can continual physical tension possibly do anything except *destroy* my concentration?'

I'm taken aback by your knowledge (and by your perfectly sound logic), so I decide on another approach. I tell you that smoking will make you more confident. Immediately, you say:

'I don't think so. Are you telling me that I'll be more confident when I've got yellow teeth, stinking breath and eyes like dropped blood samples?'

THAT'S WHY I know you're going to lose all interest in smoking cigarettes. Because, by explaining the position you're really in, I'm going to show you how to get up off your knees.

Now I'm really shaken, but I decide to have one more go. I tell you that smoking will help you lose weight (maybe you're not overweight, but just imagine you are for the purposes of this). Immediately, you say:

'I don't think so. I can lose weight by cutting out one meal a day and doing some exercise – or at least I can while I've not had my arms and legs amputated because of smoking.'

Stop the clock.

Stand back and ask yourself a question:

Why do so many smokers claim to believe this bullshit?

The answer is depressingly simple. They weren't asked to believe it *before* they started smoking, but *afterwards* when they no longer had a choice.

Don't forget that, as a cigarette salesman, I work for one of the most dishonest and cynical industries on the face of the planet. Do you really think I'd unleash these 'unique selling points' on you before you started smoking? Do you honestly believe I'd be stupid enough to let you argue with me from a position of strength, or do you think I'd force you to your knees first?

That's why I know you're going to lose all interest in smoking cigarettes. Because, by explaining the position you're really in, I'm going to show you how to get up off your knees. And make no mistake, right from the moment you smoked your second cigarette, that's where you were, *on your knees*, *tricked*, *deceived*, *frightened*, *outsmarted*, just like I was.

* * * * *

Think back to the very beginning of your affair with cigarettes. Were you ever given the real facts before you started smoking? Did the cigarette industry ever have the decency and honesty to send a couple of their senior people round to see you when you were eleven, and say…

'Hello. I'm Mr Benson and this is Mr Hedges. We're from the Golden Polonium cigarette company. The thing is, we'd like you to throw away your money, your health, your self-esteem and eventually your life, on a product that will create *a permanent state of chemically induced anxiety*,

BUT CAN YOU now sense a door quietly opening up for you somewhere deep inside your head?

a product that will inconvenience and humiliate you thousands of times before you finally drop dead – twenty years early. Incidentally, this product contains a lethal radioactive element called polonium-210, which will leak radiation inside your lungs. When they cremate you, your ashes will glow in the dark. Sign here please.'

Are you angry?

Are you *embarrassed*?

If you are embarrassed, good. You should be embarrassed. Why should I tell you otherwise? If the cigarette industry broke into your house and wrecked all your furniture, you'd call the police. But you've let them into *your mind*, you've let them do infinitely more damage, *and you've even paid them to do it!*

Don't worry. I've not turned against you. I'm just trying to make you see the sheer astronomical absurdity and futility of smoking for what it really is. It's a dream, a trick, an illusion, a life-long attempt to escape from an invisible cage created by smoking itself.

It's a phobia in which the only escape open to you has been creating more fear.

But can you now sense a door quietly opening up for you somewhere deep inside your head? Can you sense an escape route, an opportunity for freedom? If you can, *you don't need to rush for it just yet.*

Just keep reading.

Some smokers initially become offended and

indignant when I explain that they've fallen victim to a trick. But look at it logically – *how could smoking possibly be anything other than some type of trick?* Without some form of deception, how can any adult human being possibly be persuaded to *switch off all their survival instincts* and pay to give themselves lung cancer without even being able to explain why?

I don't know what you do for a living, but I suspect that you couldn't walk into a pub and start a public debate simply by putting your business card on the bar next to your drink.

I can.

When any smoker, no matter how shy, finds out what I do, their lives become instantly dominated by *the urge to tell me why in detail why they smoke*. Their eyes widen to the size of dinner plates with what they think is enthusiasm (it's not) as they abandon their seats and make their way

IF YOU'RE 'BETWEEN cigarettes' right now, concentrate hard on what you're feeling and you'll see that everything I've been telling you is true.

to the bar with their cover stories, always delivered with the same desperation that pours from the brain of every smoker on the planet.

I'm still waiting for someone to tell me that they smoke because they want to rid the world of cigarettes, or that they smoke because they believe that polonium-210 will protect them from ghosts, but it's always the same things over and over again, exactly the same stuff that I used to cling to.

* * * * *

Before getting stuck into the first cover story, let's remind ourselves once again of why you smoke. This fact will protect you for the rest of your life, but only when you're absolutely, totally confident in it. So let's make sure you are.

The nicotine in cigarette smoke causes a delayed feeling of physical tension, which your subconscious mind mistakes for fear or anxiety. Smoking, while creating this tension, briefly reduces it first. This tricks your subconscious mind into believing that smoking makes you more relaxed. But smoking can't reduce genuine anxiety, it can only reduce the synthetic anxiety caused by the previous cigarette.

Just read that again. Remember that it's backed up by your own experience, dozens of scientific reports and the experience of every smoker who's ever lived. Now, I'm going to ask you to read it one more time. Read it slowly, think about it, make sure you digest it, start trying to 'feel it', match it against the last cigarette you smoked and the one before that.

If you're 'between cigarettes' right now, concentrate hard on what you're feeling and you'll see that everything I've been telling you is true. An underlying state of mild, chemically induced agitation caused by the delayed effects of nicotine. It's a vague churning sensation, a slight tightness in your chest, your neck, and the muscles round your mouth and eyes. A sickly knot in your stomach that is now so familiar that you hardly notice it.

But it's important that you allow yourself to notice it now. Understand how easily your subconscious mind could (and does) mistake this sensation for stress or fear. Also understand that it's nothing more than your body's natural delayed reaction to nicotine. It's not fear or anxiety at all. It just feels like it. It's absolutely nothing to be scared of, so start seeing it for what it really is. Take your eyes off the shadows and start looking at what's actually causing them.

Understand something else. The sensation you're feeling now doesn't mean your body wants a cigarette. *It means you had one and it didn't work!*

When you think about having a cigarette, your subconscious mind isn't thinking about the taste, the smell, or whether it will help you to avoid putting on weight. *It's imagining this feeling of fake anxiety easing, even if only briefly, when you take the first drag.* It's imagining breathing out some of that tension along with a cloud of smoke.

All it really wants is that brief period in which the feeling of tightness loosens slightly from around your chest and face, the moment that the vague knot relaxes its grip on your stomach, allowing you to be 'yourself' again – just like you were before you started smoking.

IT'S LIKE SOMEONE sticking a pin in a voodoo doll. It can only hurt you if you've been tricked into believing it's going to hurt you.

But ask yourself this. If this sensation of tension is really so bad, why have you invested so much time and money in keeping it going day and night? If it keeps burning you, why do you keep pouring petrol on it?

Because you didn't know you were. You were tricked by nicotine.

You smoke because the delayed sensation of nicotine reminds your subconscious mind of feeling nervous, it reminds you of being threatened, in danger. But, without the panic reaction, the sensation itself can't possibly hurt you, so for the first time in your life, I want you to start experimenting with the following thought:

'If I were to stop smoking, I'd continue to feel a sensation of physical tension for a few days...

... *so what?*'

As with any other phobia, it's the fear that is hurting you – the sensation itself is just the trigger. It's like someone sticking a pin in a voodoo doll. It can only hurt you if you've been tricked into *believing* it's going to hurt you. That's how voodoo works. It's a highly developed form of fear-based hypnosis. It's a phobia triggered by superstition.

So is the belief that stopping smoking is bound to be a massive struggle. It's a popular (and highly profitable) myth on a global scale. But don't just believe me, simply look at the facts with your own eyes. Take away the superstition and the mass hysteria, chase down the shadows that fuel your phobia and ask yourself what will really happen if you stop smoking? No pain, no bleeding, no dizziness, *just a continuation of the vague feeling of 'tightness' caused by the delayed effects of nicotine. That's all. And it's not even going to exist if you don't smoke for a few days.*

* * * * *

I recently recorded an audio CD specifically for businesses who have employees who want to stop smoking. I visited one company in order to explain to their smokers how best to use it, and to answer questions. During my discussion with them, one woman, a heavy smoker, made an absolutely eye-opening observation, one that I hadn't even thought of. She said:

'I wish nicotine withdrawal symptoms were *worse*. It would be so much easier to stop smoking!'

I was stunned. As bizarre as it sounds, she was absolutely right! If the delayed feeling caused by nicotine involved severe pain, or some other extreme form of suffering, smokers would find it an absolute piece of cake to stop smoking. Do you know why?

Because they'd know when it ended!

This is what makes smoking so treacherous, because it's driven by sensations so mild and painless that they can't hurt you because of how they feel, but they can hurt you because of what they feel *like*, what they remind your subconscious mind of.

The truth is, all phobias are triggered, not by situations, but by *the fear of those situations. Smoking is no different.*

IF YOU GOT food poisoning from eating a bad pizza, would you immediately go back and eat another twenty pizzas from the same place, one after another?

Until last year, I had a crippling phobia of speaking to audiences. It absolutely terrified me. But when I started doing nicotine trick workshops, I had no choice but to face it. I couldn't just hide in a big cardboard box with a microphone and speak to groups of smokers without them seeing me. It would hardly have inspired confidence, particularly as I was there to explain that smoking is a phobia.

When I faced my own phobia down by speaking at my first workshop, I realised that I actually love speaking to groups of people, particularly about the nicotine trick. So what had I been so scared of? In fact, I hadn't been scared of speaking to audiences all along. What I'd been scared of was what speaking to an audience *represented* – vulnerability and possible rejection.

In essence, all phobias are the same. They're *fear of the unknown*.

The question of whether something frightens you or not is all about what you know, how certain you are. If you eat a bad pizza, or drink a bad pint, you'll feel ill an hour or so later. You may feel nauseous, your stomach might hurt, but it won't cause you to panic, because…. *you'll know what caused it. There's no fear because there's no confusion.*

> IT DOESN'T MATTER how much you shake your head, thinking that it must be more complicated than this. It isn't more complicated than this! *It's simple, simple, simple!*

If you got food poisoning from eating a bad pizza, would you immediately go back and eat another twenty pizzas from the same place, one after another? No. So why do you keep reacting to 'withdrawal symptoms' by giving yourself more 'withdrawal symptoms', when you could simply stop smoking and be permanently free of the entire smoking nightmare in a few days?

Because your subconscious mind isn't seeing this reality. It's seeing the chemically induced illusion. It's focusing on a single irrelevant detail (smoking briefly reduces the nicotine effect from the previous cigarette) and ignoring the important detail (smoking is the sole cause of this sensation).

The reason is that your subconscious mind mistakes this sensation for fear, which represents danger or threat. It therefore doesn't see the task of reducing it as irrelevant…

… it sees it as urgent!

Imagine that smoking a cigarette caused physical tension immediately, rather than taking about an hour. You wouldn't want to smoke again, would you?

I've got news for you. If your body is free of nicotine to start with, it does cause tension immediately, but it doesn't reach full strength for about an hour. The confusion is caused by the fact that, if you're already suffering from the delayed effects of nicotine, more nicotine will slightly reduce this sensation before you start feeling it all over again. *It's a simple illusion caused by the chemical properties of nicotine.*

It doesn't matter how much you shake your head, thinking that it must be more complicated than this. It isn't more complicated than this!

It's simple, simple, simple!

Have you ever watched a household pet do something absolutely stupid based on an obvious misunderstanding? Have you been torn between horror and amusement at the sight of a hyped-up puppy introducing its skull to a double-glazed patio door at thirty miles an hour, just because that door was open a few moments earlier?

If you're laughing, don't laugh too hard, because you've fallen for a trick that, in essence, is no more sophisticated than this. *And it's left you with more than a sore head – it's left you with a phobia that kills millions of people every year.*

Have you ever stepped aside from the mass hysteria about stopping smoking and asked yourself exactly what a 'craving' really is? This mythical word is continually bandied around without any explanation whatsoever, as though it's something that falls out of the sky and just 'happens' to smokers for no reason whatsoever. But nothing could be further from the truth. You've never wanted a cigarette for a 'random' reason. You've wanted it because your sub-conscious mind was frightened by the delayed effects of nicotine, and felt that smoking a cigarette would make you calmer and less anxious. Your body doesn't want nicotine. In fact, *there's no such thing as a physical craving for anything. It doesn't exist.*

IN THE MIND of someone suffering from an eating disorder, this abnormal reaction to food actually 'feels' normal, in the same way that smoking a cigarette eventually 'feels' normal to a smoker.

Yes, you did read that correctly. There is no such thing as a physical craving. *Your body isn't capable of 'wanting' something, any more than your video recorder is capable of 'wanting' you to play a particular film in it.* Only your subconscious mind can crave something, whether it's a cigarette, sex, a bet in the bookies, or even a meal.

Surely this can't be true. What about hunger? The craving for food is physical, isn't it? Actually, no it isn't. If the craving for food were physical, why is half the western world overweight? If hunger were purely physical, the body would only crave food when it needed it. The fact that so many people are overweight proves that it's the mind that craves food. *It can be tricked into being 'hungry'.* That's why food advertising is a multi-billion-dollar industry. Because, put simply, *it works*.

Of course, the body *triggers* the desire for food by sending strong physical signals to the brain whenever it's low on energy, but *it's your subconscious brain that actually interprets these as hunger* and decides to tell you to eat. If someone has *anorexia* or *bulimia*, exactly the same physical sensations are being sent to the brain by the body, but the subconscious mind is reacting illogically to these signals – they don't 'mean' what they should. But, in the mind of someone suffering from an eating disorder, this abnormal reaction to food actually 'feels' normal, in the same way that smoking a cigarette eventually 'feels' normal to a smoker.

The contradictory properties of nicotine have caused your subconscious brain to misunderstand the delayed sensation of nicotine and react illogically – by smoking.

That's the trick. That's how it really works. Now let's look at the cover-up that hides it, starting with the first cover story: *smoking helps you to concentrate.*

Cover Story One – Smoking helps me concentrate

Did you know that the number-one cause of houses burning down is people carelessly discarding cigarettes?

In other words, people smoking without concentrating properly.

Strange really, if smoking improves concentration.

Anyway, what actually *is* 'concentration'? Concentration is simply the ability to focus on a task. Let's take one situation in which you would need to concentrate.

Let's say you're filling in a boring official form. In fact, you're so bored, at this second, you feel that, if you were about to die, *someone else's* life would flash in front of you. But it's not a major problem. The questions are tedious, but not difficult. You're a smoker, but you're quite comfortable at this moment (or as comfortable as a smoker ever can be). You just want to get the form completed so you can do something that is a bit more fun.

Then it happens. You suddenly get an awkward, unexpected question. Maybe it's asking for a piece of information you don't quite understand, or maybe it seems to be one of those questions designed to wheedle something out of you against your will.

BUT, IF YOU haven't got nicotine-induced tension in the first place, how exactly have you reduced the stress by smoking? You haven't.

What happens?

What happens is this. Your mind suddenly feels worried, and *your body reacts as it always has done –* *by feeling physically tense.* Your concentration is now gone, so what do you do? Well, if you're like most smokers, you have a cigarette. But what does it achieve? Well, if you've got nicotine-induced tension, it reduces this feeling for a little while, and your subconscious mind briefly feels less 'frightened'.

But, if you haven't got nicotine-induced tension in the first place, how exactly have you reduced the stress by smoking? You haven't. Even official scientific reports state clearly that *nicotine does not reduce genuine stress in the slightest.* (If it did, there'd be no need to spend billions developing drugs like Prozac and Valium.)

Has the cigarette magically filled in the right answer for you? Has the nicotine inspired you to remember a piece of crucial information? No. *All you've done is sow the seeds of full-blown physical tension in about an hour's time.*

The biggest problem I face when exposing this particular cover story, is that the truth is so spectacularly opposite to the cover story that it's difficult to avoid going overboard attacking it. The reason smokers believe that smoking aids concentration is, ironically, that *smoking destroys concentration.* If this sounds like a contradiction, you need to look at the facts again.

If you feel a sensation that your brain mistakes for stress or fear, of course it destroys your ability to concentrate on what you were doing – that's the entire purpose of fear. *It's there to make you deal with a perceived threat, so why would it let you concentrate on what you were already doing?*

But, as surprising as it may sound, your concentration hasn't been destroyed by the sensation at all. It's been destroyed by the fact that *your brain has confused the sensation with genuine stress or fear.* Millions of people concentrate perfectly well while suffering far bigger problems than the vague sensation of tension caused by nicotine. What about deaf people? What about blind people? What about people who spend their lives suffering from arthritis or tinnitus, or one of a thousand more problematic conditions than the painless physical tension you get from smoking?

Your subconscious mind keeps crying out for more nicotine for two reasons. Firstly, it interprets the delayed sensation caused by nicotine as fear *because that's what it feels like*. Secondly, as a result of the confusing time delay between the cigarette and the tension, it misses the fact that *smoking is the sole cause of this sensation*.

> WHEN MY MIND thinks of smoking, it automatically knows what the result of it would be – a total absence of pleasure or relaxation followed by a delayed feeling of tension that would then last about four days before fading away permanently.

By the time you end your affair with cigarettes, this simply won't be the case any more. Your subconscious mind will know that this sensation will be restarted if you smoke another cigarette. It will also know that, even though the delayed effects of nicotine feel like stress or fear, they're nothing of the kind. You'll therefore feel no need to panic or to create a fake explanation for this sensation, because you'll know the reason for it – smoking.

I used to respond to almost everything by

lighting up. It was absolutely ridiculous. When I had a beer, when I had a coffee, when I had an argument, when I watched a film, when I played pool, when I played cards, when I was trying to impress a woman on a date. My desire to smoke was like a *nicotine hair-trigger*. Now, absolutely nothing can trigger a desire to smoke. It's not because I'm strong, or because I have willpower, and it's certainly not because I'm particularly clever (which, I promise you, I'm not – I've struggled for more than a year to write this book!). It's got nothing to do with any of this. It's quite simply that when my mind thinks of smoking, it automatically knows what the result of it would be – *a total absence of pleasure or relaxation followed by a delayed feeling of tension that would then last about four days before fading away permanently.*

WHILE YOU'RE A smoker, time and time again you're missing those extra few moments of crucial footage. Millions upon millions of smokers have died without seeing them.

* * * * *

A smoker recently asked me 'This is all very well, but what will I do in future instead of smoking? I hate to admit it, but I immediately burst out laughing and was forced to apologise. It wasn't so much the question, it was the hangdog facial expression which accompanied it, as though breathing smoke in order to get nicotine were the most natural thing in the world. In fact, it's a perfectly reasonable question to someone whose mind believes that smoking is a natural reaction to stress.

So here's the answer. As a smoker, whenever the idea of a cigarette occurs to you, there are two possibilities. Either you can smoke, or you can't smoke. If you can't smoke (let's say you're in a meeting, or on a plane, or in a non-smoker's car), the fake chemical stress is immediately joined by real stress because you can't smoke. On the other hand, if you can smoke, you're forced to go through the hassle of physically smoking, in order to simply 'reset' a feeling of chemical stress to a lower level, which will then instantly start growing all over again. Either way, you end up stressed as a result of thinking about cigarettes.

Here's what happens to me. Whenever the idea of a cigarette even enters my head, I get an immediate feeling of immense relief and pleasure that I'm no longer under the spell of the nicotine trick, and that I no longer have the underlying feeling of chemical tension caused by smoking. This intensely pleasurable thought causes stress-reducing chemicals to be released into my bloodstream. In other words, *I have physically done something instead of smoking.* I've taken massive pleasure from the idea of cigarettes, in a way which I never once achieved in twenty years of smoking. What's more, I can do it in the middle of a meeting, I can do it on a plane, it costs absolutely nothing, and it happens as an automatic result of exactly the same mental impulse which used to cause me to smoke. Even better, I can enjoy it a thousand times in a single day if I want. How many cigarettes could you smoke in a day, even if they worked? Exactly. That's why I make a point of thinking about cigarettes as much as possible!

Have you ever seen that TV advert where you're shown part of a scene in which a man sprints towards another man and wrestles him to the ground? It appears that a vicious attack has just taken place. Then the scene is shown again *for a split second longer*. This time, immediately after the man is wrestled to the ground, a huge crate smashes into the ground where he was standing a moment previously. The first man wasn't attacking him at all – *he was saving his life*!

The entire meaning of what just happened is changed by a single moment of extra knowledge. Suddenly, you 'feel' differently about the first man – he's not a thug, he's a hero!

While you're a smoker, time and time again you're missing those extra few moments of crucial footage. Millions upon millions of smokers have died without seeing them. All they ever saw was the moment where the chemically induced tension eased slightly after the first drag of a cigarette. But they completely missed what happened afterwards. *They failed to see that the sensation of physical tension was caused by smoking every single time.* They died trapped inside a cage of ignorance. Every time they ever smoked, their subconscious minds reacted perfectly, but *only to a tiny, isolated part of the picture*.

And it killed them. They died trying to rid themselves of a sensation that would have gone away by itself in about four days if only they'd stopped smoking! What a ludicrous situation to actually die from such a simple misunderstanding!

The billions of dollars spent each year by the tobacco industry is being spent swamping you with images that have one purpose and one purpose only – to make sure that, *under no circumstances will your subconscious brain ever be allowed to see that critical extra footage, the footage you've now seen in this book.* But, unfortunately for them...

... it's too late. You've seen it.

Let's look at the next cover story.

Cover Story Two – Smoking Makes Me Confident

A few years ago, I was out of work for six months, during which time I became exceedingly overweight after developing a highly unfortunate fascination with pizzas. This was no problem for me because, as a smoker, I knew I was damaging myself so much with cigarettes that pizzas would only increase my chances of dying young very slightly. It's one of the shining advantages of smoking.

Every few days, I would start salivating like a rabid dog and I'd phone the local pizza place to order a seventeen-inch 'Cardiac Surprise' (or something similar) with extra pepperoni. I'd wash it down (or as far down as it would go) with an ocean of beer and then I'd celebrate this momentous achievement with a cigarette.

After just a few weeks, I began to realise that something strange was happening to my washing machine. I know it sounds strange, but it seemed to be selectively shrinking all my trousers and under-pants, while leaving my socks exactly the same size. Even weirder, it was shrinking just the collars on my shirts without touching the cuffs or sleeves. It was a technical fault I have never encountered before or since. Ever the optimist, I managed to persuade myself that I was the victim of nothing more sinister than cheap Taiwanese engineering.

> WHY WOULD BEING a pathetic, cringing, confused, outsmarted cigarette smoker make anyone feel confident?

Just like my 'physique', the situation was destined to go pear-shaped. A few weeks later, I was walking around in the local town centre, and I suddenly walked straight into an ex-girlfriend, one I hadn't seen for several years. You must understand that when I was seeing this girl, I'd been almost two stone lighter and in gainful employment. She stammered something at me, I stammered something at her, and we both blushed. I knew that she was shocked by my lard-stricken appearance, and I was equally mortified that she was there to see it. After a semi-mumbled conversation, we parted and I immediately smoked two cigarettes.

Why? It was the domino (or 'Domino's') effect. My shattered confidence made me feel anxious…

… my subconscious mind concluded that smoking would make me feel less anxious…

… so I smoked.

On the positive side, my pizza fixation was fixed. The next day, I started cautiously dieting (although the smoking made it impossible for me to exercise). As an added bonus, my washing machine began to get better by itself.

Why would being a pathetic, cringing, confused, outsmarted cigarette smoker make anyone feel confident? Why would any human being feel good about falling for a trick so mundane that even lab rats can't be forced to fall for it?

Why would anyone believe the Hollywood image of Bruce Willis in *Die Hard*, or Kim Basinger in *LA Confidential*? Do you really think most movie stars smoke in real life? Why do you think Los Angeles has one of the lowest rates of smoking anywhere in the world?

BUT WHAY SORT of life is so fragile that running out of cigarettes can turn it into a total nightmare?

Because they're obsessed with their looks. Either get with the programme or prepare to take the consequences. Take responsibility for your own mind or the tobacco industry will be more than happy to do it for you.

When you're smoking a cigarette, you're not demonstrating *independence, courage or poise*. You're demonstrating *stupidity, anxiety and weakness. You're putting your phobia on show for the entire world to see. Is that how you want to live the rest of your life?*

Beating the nicotine trick is the best thing I've ever done in my life. Beating the nicotine trick didn't just give me the information needed to write this book, it also gave me the confidence. I had no confidence before. I had no reason for confidence. Okay, I had friends, I had my (somewhat bizarre) sense of humour, I had my 'life'. But what sort of life is so fragile that running out of cigarettes can turn it into a total nightmare?

What sort of life has you terrified of getting a sore throat because you know you'll be forced to make it even worse with smoking?

What sort of life has you continually forced to plan for the next cigarette and desperate to avoid situations that will expose your stupidity, gullibility and weakness?

What sort of life has you forced to lie to yourself every single day?

What sort of life has you wondering whether the next cigarette will be the one that starts lung cancer?

What sort of life has you looking over your shoulder year after year waiting for a shadowy figure to put his hand on your arm?

Confidence? From smoking?

Get real.

I now have the confidence to shake hands with people who have smoked tens of thousands of cigarettes, look them in the eyes and tell them I can finally explain why they're doing it.

Let's take a look at the next cover story.

Cover Story Three – Smoking Stops Me Putting on Weight

This is an absolute beauty. When a smoker looks at me and says…

'I'll put on weight if I stop smoking… '

… I always feel a strange sense of unreality. It's like speaking to a person *inside* a person. When smokers say this to me, there is always a look in their eyes, one that seems to plead with me, one that seems to say…

'*… please stop me believing this lunacy!*'

So let me do just that.

When you were born, you weighed just a few pounds, so it's safe to say that most of the weight you've 'put on' in your life has been harmless. But when smokers talk about putting on weight in the context of stopping smoking, what they really mean is that they're scared of overeating.

So let's take a look at this. There are two main reasons why people don't want to

> WHICH DO YOU think your body is more capable of dealing with – a few extra pounds under your belt, or a combination of nicotine, carbon monoxide, polonium-210, lead, nickel and benzene in your lungs twenty times each day?

overeat. One is vanity and the other is fear of the health consequences. But, if you're a smoker, *surely you've already proved that neither of these matter to you, so why would you be scared of putting on weight?*

Think about it. If you smoke, your breath stinks (whatever you think), your skin is damaged, your eyes are dull, your hair has been stripped of nutrients, and your 'habit' is an object of disgust and embarrassment to most non-smokers. So why do you care about putting on weight, whether it's a result of stopping smoking or anything else? Why would being over-

SMOKERS ARE SCARED because their subconscious minds mistake the delayed reaction to nicotine for fear, and because the time delay makes them fail to see this sensation as the direct result of smoking.

weight be worse than inhaling radioactive smoke into your lungs, and exhaling the residue all over other people?

But, you might say, *what about the health risks of being overweight?*

I've got news for you. You could stop smoking, deteriorate into a wet-mouthed, shame-faced, pizza-eating slob (like I once did) and *still be healthier than you are now*. Which do you think your body is more capable of dealing with – a few extra pounds under your belt, or a combination of nicotine, carbon monoxide, polonium-210, lead, nickel and benzene in your lungs twenty times each day? If you've ever used this excuse, think about it for a second. Are you really suggesting that you're prepared to spend the rest of your life breathing radioactive smoke simply in order to avoid putting on weight?

So, am I saying that you'll put on weight if you stop smoking? No, I'm not saying any such thing. I'm simply exposing the hollowness of the cover story. Don't forget that, by definition, a cover story isn't true. A cover story is designed, not to illuminate a truth, *but to perpetuate an illusion*.

Here's the point. If you force yourself to stop smoking without removing your phobia, you'll feel nervous, vulnerable and insecure. If you feel nervous, vulnerable and insecure, you'll look for some way to comfort yourself. If you look for some way to comfort yourself, it might be food. It might be chocolate. It might be steak and kidney pudding, chips, peas and gravy. It might be cheeseburgers. It might be raspberry milk-shakes. It might be your own nails.

But you're not going to force yourself to stop smoking. You're going to do the exact opposite. You're going to escape from the phobia, which means that each time you even think of cigarettes, you'll immediately feel the exact opposite of insecure. You won't have created an empty space, you'll have permanently filled one. Just the knowledge that you no longer feel tense from cigarettes will, by itself, be intensely pleasurable, satisfying, reassuring and comforting. And, unlike food or cigarettes, you'll be able to give yourself this secret pleasure whenever you want to, without calories, without consequences, without financial expense. Just by thinking about cigarettes.

Let's look at the final cover story.

Cover Story Four – Smoking is Just a Habit

The final cover story is different than the other three cover stories, because the other cover stories pretend to be reasons to smoke. In effect, 'it's just a habit' is essentially the claim that the smoker is smoking *for no reason at all*.

Unfortunately, rather than making it easier to dismiss this cover story, this lack of logic actually makes it more difficult, not because it makes any sense (it doesn't, as I'll prove in a second), but because of the smoker's *state of mind* when he (or she) says it.

To understand why, you need to realise that, when a smoker says that smoking is a habit, it's usually after he or she has exhausted all the other cover stories, and has come to the conclusion that there's just no point even worrying about smoking any more. It's a form of denial. It means: 'I don't know and I don't want to know.'

But let's dig a bit deeper.

Interestingly, the dictionary definition of a habit is simply '*an activity that is continually repeated*'. Technically, therefore, smoking *is* a habit in the dictionary sense. However, the suggestion is that the smoker can stop smoking whenever they want. Technically, this is also true. Then again, technically, someone who has a phobia of heights can climb up a two-hundred-foot crane, balance to the end of it and then abseil down to the ground using their shoelaces.

Technically.

Let me describe another habit, then we'll compare it with smoking and see what happens.

While you're in a job, you get up, get dressed and go to work as a matter of habit. You go to the same place each day as a matter of habit. You speak to the same people each day as a matter of habit. You park your car, or catch a particular train, as a matter of habit. You have each weekend off as a matter of habit (if you don't, you have my sympathies). You get lunch somewhere regularly, as a matter of habit.

But, if you were made redundant, or moved to a different job…

… would you keep turning up at your old job out of habit?

… would you keep getting the train to where you used to work out of habit?

> IF YOU KEEP smoking, you'll be forced to keep one or more of these cover stories going for the rest of your life.

… would you keep giving people your old business card out of habit?

Of course not. Even though these are all deeply ingrained habits, they only exist *while there's a reason for them to exist*. Without this reason, it's easy to let go of literally hundreds of

habits that are all connected to something you
don't need to do anymore. In fact, *it's so easy that
it doesn't even occur to you that you've done it.*

With smoking, not only do you need to buy
cigarettes, get an ashtray, find somewhere to
smoke, possibly get permission, and so on, but on
top of all this you then need
to *go directly against all your
natural survival instincts,*
simply in order to smoke.

THAT'S WHY IT won't
fail. Because, believe
it or not, your
subconscious mind
has never failed.

But there's something else
that exposes this cover story
as false. Let's say that you walk to the newsagents
each day using a particular route, as a matter of
'habit'. One morning, you discover that a mains
pipe has flooded the road and you can't follow
that particular route anymore.

Do you immediately panic? Do you start
sweating? Do you beg a friend to give you a piggy-
back through the water? Do you react with blind
panic, like you do when…

… *you can't smoke?*

No. Smoking is not a habit. You smoke because
your subconscious mind wants you to. And it
wants you to because it confuses the delayed
sensation of nicotine with fear, and vice versa.

You smoke because you have a phobia. Period.

* * * * *

Many smokers who are thinking of quitting tend to fixate on all the things they think they believe – the cover stories – and they assume they'll need to somehow find a way of 'defeating' all of them separately before stopping. They think they'll want to smoke when they drink, they believe they'll want to smoke when they go to a wedding or a funeral, they believe their lives will never be the same without cigarettes.

When a smoker believes this, is it any wonder that quitting smoking seems like an overwhelming task? I've seen grown men and women reduced to tears as they've talked about the struggle they've had with cigarettes. But the reason they failed was because *they were never struggling with cigarettes or even struggling against withdrawal symptoms.*

Without knowing it, they were actually struggling against their own subconscious mind!

That's why they never stood a chance. You can't override your own subconscious mind. It's not designed to be overridden, by you or anyone else. *But I repeat – you're not going to try to.*

You're not going to force yourself to stop smoking this time. You're simply going to make your subconscious mind see the truth about smoking, and let it make the decision for you.

That's why it won't fail. Because, believe it or not, your subconscious mind has never failed. Even when it's been telling you to smoke, it's been doing the right thing, but based on *false information*. By the time it lets go of smoking, it will still be doing the right thing, but based on *correct information*.

In fact, I'm not going to tell you to smoke a 'last cigarette' or even suggest that you set a date for stopping smoking. It doesn't work like that, as I've been explaining all the way through this book. I'm simply going to help you to naturally lose the fear response that drives your smoking. It's going to happen automatically. So just enjoy it. Think of it as a jigsaw with just a few pieces missing. They're the most enjoyable bit of the whole experience.

Even if you throw this book away right now, a cigarette will never feel the same for you again. Even as you read this sentence, your subconscious mind is finally starting to wise up to the nicotine trick. If you don't believe me, feel free to test it with a cigarette whenever you want. You'll find that it feels 'different', somehow *even more disappointing* than before. You'll also be more aware than that there is absolutely *no pleasure whatsoever* to be had from smoking a cigarette. None at all.

You'll also realise that the underlying feeling of tension isn't completely removed even if you inhale more deeply than you ever have before. In fact, if you concentrate really hard, you'll notice that you can feel that unnatural sense of chemical tension even now, as you read this sentence.

Enjoy it while it lasts.

If you keep smoking, you'll be forced to keep one or more of these cover stories going for the rest of your life. You haven't got time for that. You've got a life to live. Very shortly, I'm going to show you specifically how your subconscious mind is going to start seeing smoking as an *anti-climax*. But first, there's one final issue you need to be straight on.

Cigarettes and Alcohol

Cigarettes and alcohol. It has a certain festive ring, don't you think?

Cigarettes and alcohol.

Parties and fun.

Dancing and music.

Christmas and New Year.

Cirrhosis and lung cancer.

There he goes again. Typical Neil Casey. Spoiling the fun. Why does he always have to pour cold water on everything? What's wrong with him? Doesn't he know the rest of us have real jobs, with real pressures? Doesn't he know that most people don't spend their lives writing books, recording CDs, and lecturing smokers? Who can blame people for letting their hair down at times? After all…

… you could get hit by a bus tomorrow.

True.

You could get hit by a bus today, for that matter. I met a man at an early nicotine trick workshop who was immensely proud of the fact that he was a heavy drinker and heavy smoker, and even more proud of the fact that he'd never made any attempt to cut down on either booze or fags. He was only sixty, but already he was starting to look like…

… he'd been hit by a bus.

Still, whatever makes people happy, right?

But that's the point. *He wasn't happy*. The fear was like red fire behind his eyes. But aren't cigarettes and alcohol supposed to drive away fear? Doesn't life teach us to see these things either as a reward, or as a pick-me-up?

The relaxing cigarette after sex.

The large brandy after a sudden shock.

The champagne breakfast.

The celebratory cigar.

Is it any wonder that the link between smoking and drinking is so strong?

There's another thing that smoking and drinking have in common, and that's the strange fact that we unknowingly refer to each of these activities in a very vague way. How many times have you heard someone who's about to have a drink say:

BY PUTTING A friendly or off-hand slant on activities like drinking and smoking, we allow ourselves to take a different view of them, we allow ourselves to see them as just a 'bit of fun', a way of 'letting go'.

'I'm just going to ingest several millilitres of alcohol. For an optimal, two-hour period, this will cause my fine motor coordination to be impaired and I'll feel less inhibited socially. This will enable me to engage in conversations with

people in whose company I normally feel insecure. Unfortunately, there will also be the possibility of me becoming either embarrassingly flirtatious or unnecessarily argumentative, although I feel this risk is justified under the circumstances.'

Huh?

You wouldn't hear it from doctors, surgeons or even subscribers to *Crossword Monthly*. People say things like:

'I'm just going for a drink'. Or maybe they don't even mention drinking at all. Maybe they just say:

'I'm going out for a couple of hours.'

The same applies with smoking. Have you ever noticed the almost unspoken code that passes between smokers who are planning a fag break? It's all little nods and winks and meaningful glances at the door. Have you ever said to another smoker:

'I've got a great idea. Why don't we inhale a tiny amount of nicotine into our lungs. This will make the tension from the previous cigarette we smoked go away slightly, although obviously it will cause this tension to start building all over again, which I suppose makes it a complete waste of time.'

No. Instead you say (or mime):

'Cigarette?'

By putting a friendly or off-hand slant on activities like drinking and smoking, we allow ourselves to take a different view of them, we allow ourselves to see them as just a 'bit of fun', a way of 'letting go'.

In case you believe I'm some kind of health freak since I discovered the nicotine trick, let me tell you that last night I ate an enormous amount of Chinese food from a questionable local take-away (ominously nicknamed the 'Di Yung'). I then drank several pints of lager, sat in front of the television until midnight, and thoroughly enjoyed myself doing it. I'm not anti-drinking and, believe it or not, I'm not even anti-smoking.

I'm anti-bullshit. Anti-deception. Anti-delusion.

I was initially dubious as to whether I should even write this section. I wanted this book to provide nothing more than the necessary information on the phobia known as the nicotine trick. But, based on what I've heard from recent workshops, it was obvious that this chapter needed to be here, for one reason:

Alcohol seems to ruin so many attempts to stop smoking.

To be more precise, millions of people stop

smoking, and then start again when they have a drink. Alcohol hasn't really ruined anything. But it's been an unwitting accessory. You need to know why alcohol is involved in so many failed attempts, and you need to know why it won't happen this time.

Firstly, remember that most attempts to stop smoking are based on a hopelessly ineffective combination of *willpower and other people's scare tactics*. In other words, the smoker is stopping, not because his or her subconscious mind has let go of the false beliefs that drive smoking, but because they think *they shouldn't smoke*. This is an absolute disaster, because all it takes is *one weak moment when the risks of smoking don't seem so bad*, and the smoker is smoking again. And what's the single biggest time when we're likely to ignore risks?

When we've had a drink!

When we're drunk, we're less concerned about danger, which is why so many fights, divorces and airborne cars happen as a result of drinking alcohol. This means that, if you force yourself to stop smoking because of the health risks, you'll be tempted to have a smoke when you drink because, at some point, you won't care about the danger of lighting up again.

The other thing is, *alcohol acts as a strong local anaesthetic*. It numbs the tongue and throat. This means that any cigarettes you've smoked when you've been drinking alcohol have physically been slightly less irritating, so your subconscious mind remembers these cigarettes as being less unpleasant than others.

ONE THING I'VE noticed is that not one smoker has ever told me they enjoy smoking while they were physically smoking a cigarette.

But this time, you're not going to stop smoking and then simply hope for the best. You're going to make your subconscious mind aware of the reality of smoking, in such a way that *it will let go of smoking for you*.

This means that, even if you get drunk after you've stopped smoking, the underlying phobia still won't be there and without that phobia your subconscious mind won't tell you to smoke.

Have you ever been tempted to pour petrol over yourself and set light to it just because you were drunk? Of course not. This impulse has never occurred to you whether you've been drunk or sober. Even when you're drunk, you can only want to smoke *if the hidden connections are being made that tell you to smoke*.

* * * * *

All the way through this book, I've been getting you to think of smoking alternately as a *one-sided affair* and a *phobia*. But surely it can't be both. Isn't this a contradiction? No, *because many one-sided affairs are effectively phobias.*

They're relationships based on fear, usually the fear of being alone or the fear of the consequences of ending the affair. In either case, if you remove the source of the fear, you remove the fear itself.

* * * * *

Smokers aren't scared of putting on weight. Smokers aren't scared of losing their confidence. Smokers aren't scared of losing their concentration. Smokers don't have a chronic physical addiction to nicotine, or an oral fixation, or 'addictive personalities', or self-destructive DNA, or horns in the middle of their heads, or anything other than *a phobia* of the delayed response to nicotine, a phobia caused by *two easily removed misunderstandings in their subconscious minds*.

Smokers are scared because their subconscious minds mistake the delayed reaction to nicotine for fear, and because the time delay makes them fail to see this sensation as the direct result of smoking.

The rest of it is bullshit, white noise, a collection of red herrings. Keep your eyes on the phobia itself, don't distract yourself with the trivia. When the phobia goes, all the other stuff will disappear by itself.

It's all a lot simpler now you know that smoking is a *phobia* rather than an *addiction* or a *habit*, because you can now start to concentrate your attention on the specific source of the fear, rather than on the side issues that just confuse things.

YOU MIGHT FIND it hard to believe that your mind can possibly let go of such an 'ingrained' reaction as smoking this easily, but it can and it will.

Our woman with the phobia of dogs doesn't panic at the sight of a cat. She doesn't panic at the sight of a cow or a horse or a giraffe. Her subconscious mind reacts specifically to dogs because it thinks that dogs are a danger to her, based on her childhood experience. In other words, *there is a specific, understandable explanation for her phobia.*

Exactly the same applies with smoking. Your

subconscious mind reacts to the physical tension caused by nicotine *because it thinks it represents a danger to you.* By telling you to smoke, it's really trying to remove fear. But once you've made your subconscious mind see that the physical tension caused by nicotine is simply a chemical sensation that *feels* like fear, a panic response will no longer makes sense and your subconscious mind will discard smoking without any willpower or hassle.

By the way, this is established science, not some way out theory. It's precisely how clinical psychologists treat people who have other phobias. There are two main methods based on the same principle. The first method is to hypnotise the sufferer and break the link between the source of fear and the fear itself. The second method is to gradually expose the sufferer to the source of the fear and let the subconscious mind see that the threat is false, at which point it will let go of the phobia by itself. Either way, the end result is the same – *the subconscious mind no longer reacts in the same way to a particular situation or sensation because it no longer sees it as a threat.*

We're going to use a variation of the second

method. In the final chapter, *I'll show you how to gently remove the fear response that drives your smoking*. You're going to make your subconscious mind understand the delayed physical tension caused by smoking for what it really is – a painless, chemically induced sensation that is directly caused by smoking a cigarette. When it sees the reality of this situation, it will stop telling you to smoke.

You might find it hard to believe that your mind can possibly let go of such an 'ingrained' reaction as smoking this easily, but *it can and it will*. Your subconscious mind will let go of even the most terrifying fear in a single moment of realisation, *provided it is given sufficient proof that the threat is no longer real*.

> HOW MANY TIMES in your life have you laughed at something that absolutely terrified you just a few seconds earlier? How much effort did it take to go from being frightened to being amused? How much willpower did it take?

But don't take my word for this. Let me prove it to you beyond all doubt.

If you walked into the room of a country mansion and suddenly saw *a huge bear with its mouth open and its teeth bared towards you*, you'd probably recoil with fear. But as soon as you realised that the bear was just a stuffed exhibit, *it would immediately cease to frighten you*, and your subconscious mind would relax and stop telling you to run away. It wouldn't take willpower, it wouldn't take hypnotism, it wouldn't take a 900-page book, or a video, or acupuncture, or thousands of pounds of therapy at a Harley Street clinic.

All it would take would be the split second in which the reality of the situation is effortlessly transferred to your subconscious mind. Make sure you understand that it really would happen this quickly and that it would take absolutely no effort.

How many times in your life have you laughed at something that absolutely terrified you just a few seconds earlier? How much effort did it take to go from being frightened to being amused? How much willpower did it take?

None. All it took was knowledge. Let me repeat that.

All it took was knowledge.

Fear and threat are things most people don't spend much time thinking about, because they're handled automatically by their subconscious minds. Even so, it's worth taking a moment to understand the difference between *threat* and *fear*. One is *the cause* and the other is *the effect*.

Do you see people running around screaming in fear at zoos because of all the dangerous wild animals in there? No, because even the most 'dangerous' wild animals represent *no threat* while they're behind bars.

But, if a twelve-foot tiger were to escape from its compound, everyone would panic, including you. Now understand this. That tiger would be exactly the same animal into whose razor-toothed face you were cheerfully pointing your Polaroid camera ten seconds earlier. But suddenly, you're more terrified than the two-year-old girl sitting in her pram nearby.

WHEN A SMOKER says that smoking is a habit, it's usually after he or she has exhausted all the other cover stories.

But, if the tiger is so 'dangerous', why weren't you scared *before* it escaped?

Because your subconscious mind has no reason to be frightened of a tiger *while it represents no threat*, so it doesn't bother to react. Why should it?

When you stop smoking this time, the physical tension caused by smoking will no longer be perceived by your subconscious mind as a threat, and it therefore won't see any need to keep triggering a panic response (i.e. smoking), because a panic response will no longer make sense to it.

Why should it?

This is why you won't need willpower, because you're not going to consciously stop smoking. You're simply going to give your subconscious mind the correct perception of what cigarettes really do, and let it stop smoking for you.

Here's a fascinating thing that I've noticed while doing nicotine trick workshops. If I ask a smoker why they smoke, they give the usual variety of answers (they enjoy it, they're addicted to nicotine, it's a habit, and so on).

But one thing I've noticed is that *not one smoker has ever told me they enjoy smoking while they were physically smoking a cigarette.*

They've only ever claimed to enjoy smoking while they've not actually been smoking.

Do you know what this means? It means that, in between cigarettes, the smoker's mind 'blanks out' the real reason for smoking a cigarette, *it tries to pretend that the phobia doesn't exist.*

This is a natural protection mechanism and, interestingly, it's a characteristic of many other phobias. They only 'kick in' when the individual detects a possible threat, and are then 'put aside' as though they didn't exist. With smoking, smokers claim to enjoy smoking because they don't even consciously know they have a phobia, so they assume that smoking must *somehow* be pleasurable.

In the final chapter of this book, we're finally going to allow your subconscious mind to face up to this phobia and defeat it. We're going to make sure your subconscious mind sees each cigarette as an… *anti-climax*.

Part Three –
Anti-Climax

Smoke and Mirrors

Let's go back to the beginning, just for a few moments.

If you're a smoker, according to the statistics, you probably want to stop smoking. But sometimes smokers tell me they want to stop smoking, and then interrupt me at every opportunity, in case I tell them something they don't want to hear. The truth is, most smokers don't want to stop smoking in the slightest, which explains why they're still smoking. They just say they want to stop smoking because they'd feel stupid saying otherwise.

> MOST SMOKERS DON'T want to stop smoking in the slightest, which explains why they're still smoking.

I recently took a phone call from a woman who said she wanted to come to a nicotine trick workshop. She sounded a bit hesitant, so I asked her if she wanted to stop smoking. Word for word, here was her reply:

'Yes. I've got to.'

I repeated the question. She repeated the reply.

'Yes. I've got to.'

Do you see what she was doing? By repeatedly qualifying the word 'yes' with the words 'I've got to', she was in effect answering a question I wasn't asking, *a question she felt more able to answer honestly.*

The question she was really answering was:

'Have you got to give up smoking?'

Of course the answer to that question is yes, unless you're already dying of lung cancer, in which case the only real risk in smoking is the risk of igniting the oxygen canister next to your bed and taking the entire hospital (and your visiting relatives) to eternity with you.

But I wasn't asking whether she *needed* to stop smoking. I was asking if she *wanted* to. She wasn't even letting my question get as far as her subconscious mind. Her voice didn't change at all. She didn't know what she was doing.

Maybe you think I'm being hard on her, but I'm simply pointing out that smokers are forced to deceive themselves all their lives. In fact, in blunt terms, the answer she was really giving was:

'No. I don't want to stop smoking.'

What most smokers really want is an excuse to carry on smoking. And if smoking wasn't so expensive, unhealthy and disgusting, they'd smoke all day, every day. This makes sense. Until they know they suffer from a *phobia*, smokers *can't* really want to stop smoking, it's impossible.

All they really want to do is get rid of the *consequences* of smoking.

And here's why. If your subconscious mind thinks you're protecting yourself from some hidden threat by smoking, why on earth would it want you to stop?

UNTIL THEY KNOW they suffer from a phobia, smokers can't really want to stop smoking, it's impossible.

Don't forget that, just like any other phobia, *smoking has now mistakenly become part of the survival instincts that help you respond to threat and danger.*

If you force yourself to stop smoking, this phobia will still be there. It won't just go away by itself. You'll feel that a crucial safety net has been taken away from you. Maybe you'll learn to live with it eventually, but it will still cast a shadow over the rest of your life.

If that was all I could offer you, do you think I'd have bothered writing this book?

No. So let's make sure you know why it's going to be different this time.

If the woman with the phobia of dogs doesn't see a dog for ten years, does that mean her phobia is cured? No. Does it mean it's simply faded away? No. All it means is that it's not been triggered. The trigger is still there, waiting to react.

It's exactly the same with smoking.

How many times has an ex-smoker told you that they still get 'cravings' months or even years after stopping?

How many times have you heard about someone who stopped smoking for years and then started again at a funeral, or during some other stressful time?

Why do you think this happens? It happens because they tried to stop smoking *without the permission of their own subconscious mind.*

This can never work in the long term. And to make this approach even more futile, whenever an ex-smoker does cave in and light up looking for relief or pleasure, the cigarette mysteriously turns its back on them and makes them feel as disappointed, dizzy, ill and stressed as their first ever cigarette did. This is because *they no longer even have the nicotine-induced sensation to partially reduce*, so, rather than the cigarette helping, they've suddenly got the tension caused by nicotine plus the tension caused by the genuine stress they were trying to relieve.

They've got double stress. What an absolute nightmare!

This is why ex-smokers are so horrified when they have a 'sudden' cigarette years after stopping. It isn't just the embarrassment and shame of smoking again. It's the *overwhelming disappointment*.

THIS IS WHY ex-smokers are so horrified when they have a 'sudden' cigarette years after stopping. It isn't just the embarrassment and shame of smoking again. It's the overwhelming disappointment.

It doesn't 'feel' like they remember at all, because any tension they've got is now caused by *genuine fear or stress*, it's no longer caused by their body's delayed reaction to nicotine, which means a cigarette can't possibly reduce it. It's like taking a headache tablet to cure indigestion. It's a misunderstanding of what the sensation actually is.

Unfortunately, what smoking a cigarette 'for old times' sake' does do is resurrect a feeling of nicotine-induced tension that the smoker's subconscious mind then *mistakes for fear and anxiety* and tries to reduce with another cigarette, and the cycle of disappointment and fear starts all over again.

Most smokers know that smoking is a waste of time, but they're not quite sure why. Survey after survey shows that almost every smoker wishes they'd never started smoking. So why don't they all just stop? Because they're in the grip of the phobia known as the nicotine trick.

Their subconscious minds aren't allowing them to stop, so they have no choice but to keep using fake reasons to keep smoking.

THE ULTIMATE CIGARETTE

What if, rather than stopping smoking, you could do the exact opposite? What if you had the opportunity to smoke *the ultimate cigarette*, a cigarette that was so powerful and satisfying that it would take *four entire days to smoke*? What if this cigarette could finally remove the feeling of physical tension caused by all the cigarettes that had gone before it, and leave you calm, satisfied and relaxed at last? What if it wasn't even going to give you a sore throat, or bad breath, or a hacking cough? And what if it wasn't going to cost you a penny?

What would you do for a cigarette like that, a cigarette that was going to finally work after all the thousands of cigarettes that haven't?

Just a fantasy, right?

Wrong. If you beat the nicotine trick, the last cigarette you ever smoke will be exactly what I've just described. It won't satisfy anything by itself, but *the fact that it's your last cigarette will.*

Over a period of about four days, the feeling of physical tension will finally fade to nothing, your craving for relief will be permanently satisfied and it won't cost you a penny. It's almost laughably simple, isn't it?

Yet, despite the truth of this, the magical four-day period following your last ever cigarette is *the single thing that terrifies most smokers who want to stop!* The hysteria about 'nicotine withdrawal symptoms' is now so widespread that smokers just don't know what to expect, so *the phobia automatically kicks in every time.*

Having helped smokers to make these four days the most enjoyable of their entire lives, this is almost unbearably frustrating for me.

How do you explain to someone who's had a feeling of physical tension for years, that the only thing that will happen if they stop smoking is that this exact same sensation will remain for a few days and then disappear? Even though it's true, it just doesn't match the overwhelming brainwashing being forced on to smokers, so it doesn't *sound* true.

In many ways, helping people to escape from the nicotine trick is like helping people to escape from a mind-control cult, a false religion that is driven by fear and blind faith in two things. Firstly, that smoking a cigarette can perform some miracle that will make you more relaxed and calm. And secondly, that leaving the religion will be a terrifying and distressing experience. Just like a real cult, it operates by tricking your normal mental process into seeing things in a distorted way.

Time after time after time, I see 'stop-smoking' books and programmes that talk about being 'strong' and having the 'power' and 'strength' to succeed, and I feel like falling to my knees and screaming in sheer frustration at the utter stupidity and ignorance of these statements. I just cannot believe that there are people whose very profession is supposedly 'smoking cessation', and *they're perpetuating exactly the same bullshit that is keeping countless millions of smokers trapped* inside their phobia, inside the invisible cage known as the nicotine trick.

Incidentally, there's another myth I need to dispel here, and that is that heavy smokers suffer stronger 'withdrawal symptoms' when they stop smoking than light smokers, that's it's somehow 'more ingrained'. In fact, there's absolutely no difference. If you smoke two drags from a single cigarette (which is enough to flood your brain with nicotine) and then stop, your body's reaction to nicotine will be exactly the same as that of a smoker who has just stubbed out their millionth cigarette. In either case, the feeling of tension is caused by *the last cigarette they smoked.*

The subconscious fear and misunderstandings that drive smoking are identical in every smoker. And the continual feeling of tension is the same whether you smoke five cigarettes each day or five hundred.

> THE SUBCONSCIOUS FEAR and misunderstandings that drive smoking are identical in every smoker. And the continual feeling of tension is the same whether you smoke five cigarettes each day or five hundred.

If your subconscious mind is mistaking the delayed effects of nicotine for fear, you're trapped by the nicotine trick. If it isn't, you're not. There are no half measures, no room for misunderstanding.

It really is this simple. Don't swallow the hype about being 'more' or 'less' hooked, or 'cutting down'. I still haven't met a single smoker who's ever succeeded in the long term by using this approach. But why would you even want to? Why would you choose reduced tension over no tension at all? Would a migraine sufferer choose a slightly reduced headache over no headache at all?

The only reason people ever look for a complicated solution to a problem is that *they don't know a simple solution exists*. When it's dark inside your house, you don't start trying to eat carrots in order to improve your eyesight so you can see in the dark. *You switch the lights on*. When it starts raining, you don't try to find some miraculous way of making it stop raining. *You pick up an umbrella*.

Why would you want to take a complicated route to becoming a non-smoker when *a blindingly simple route is directly in front of you*, like a huge illuminated runway? You've got a phobia caused by the fact that nicotine simulates fear and relaxation. It's a simple phobia, with a simple cause and an equally simple solution, which is to remove the source of the fear from your subconscious mind and then let the sensation itself die away over a four-day period.

Let me give you a specific example of how it works. A few weeks ago, a smoker got in touch with me via a mutual friend, having been told about the nicotine trick. She'd seen the 'Have you Heard?' animation on the nicotine trick web site and was in a combined state of anxiety and excitement. She was desperate to stop smoking, but worried about whether she had the willpower to do it.

Here's what I did.

After persuading her to forget about even trying to 'stop smoking', I asked her to imagine that each time she smoked a cigarette *she was being bitten by a snake and injected with mild, painless, delayed-reaction venom (nicotine)*. I got her to imagine it as vividly as she could and helped her add some extra detail to it which was meaningful to her. By doing this, she was allowing her subconscious mind to start (correctly) associating the feeling of tension caused by nicotine with *the last cigarette she smoked*.

I also gave her two simple instructions to

follow each time she smoked a cigarette, instructions that I'll explain in detail in the next section. Then I told her to smoke whenever she got even the slightest urge to. She seemed a bit disappointed by this. She was hoping I was going to 'cure' her of smoking in one sitting. I told her to give it a few days, and stressed that it was important that she followed the instructions each time she smoked.

Three days later she phoned me late in the evening. That morning, she'd woken up with a strange feeling of excitement, as though something positive had happened to her while she was asleep. She had half a packet of cigarettes on her bedside table, which no longer attracted her in the slightest. She also recognised a feeling of mild tension in her body, which she instantly knew was caused by her body's delayed reaction to nicotine. Of course, she'd known this ever since I'd explained it three days earlier, but for the first time *she really felt it*.

For the rest of the day, she waited for this sensation to trigger a desire to smoke. But, even as the feeling gradually got stronger, she had no desire to smoke. Every time she noticed the feeling of tension, *she immediately recognised it as her body's natural, delayed reaction to nicotine, a reaction she'd experienced thousands of times before.* By seeing it like this, it was *totally impossible for her to be scared by it.* After all, it wasn't hurting her in any way, and she was in no doubt as to what had caused it.

Even better, she knew without any doubt that smoking another cigarette would be like forcing the snake to bite her again. *It wouldn't hurt, but it wouldn't*

> THAT WAS THE day she finally beat the nicotine trick. Her phobia was gone. A couple of days later, she didn't even have the feeling of tension any more.

help either because her body would react to the venom all over again, causing a delayed feeling of painless physical tension. And for what? Nothing. No pleasure, no end result, nothing.

That was the day she 'got it'.

That was the day she finally beat the nicotine trick. Her phobia was gone. A couple of days later, she didn't even have the feeling of tension any more.

Remember once again that the reason the delayed response to nicotine frightens your subconscious mind so much is that *it develops gradually after you've smoked a cigarette, so it's not obvious what's caused it.*

It's called *cause and effect*. If you bang your head on a cupboard, you have a bruise. That bruise won't scare you because you know exactly what caused it. But if you were to suddenly develop a bruise on your head for no apparent reason, it would frighten the hell out of you, because… you wouldn't know how it got there.

Do 747 pilots panic when they fly into severe turbulence? No. So why do half the passengers? Because they don't know what to expect, so it takes them by surprise.

Do heart surgeons panic when they see blood? No. So why do so many patients? Because they don't know what to expect, so it takes them by surprise.

Do lion-tamers panic when they see lions? Do climbers panic when they see a sheer cliff face? Do marathon runners panic at the first sign of cramp…

… are you going to panic when you stop smoking?

Not this time. You've already got too much information to panic. Even I can't take this information off you. You can't even throw it away if you want to. You can't 'un-know' what you already know.

The way in which smokers see smoking is so upside down that sometimes it almost turns *me* upside down explaining it. That's one of the reasons I wrote this book. It allowed me to set down every element of the nicotine trick in detail and in the right order.

Let me tell you something else. The cigarette industry is absolutely delighted for you to see smoking as either 'drug addiction' or a 'habit', as long as you fail to see it as a *phobia*. And don't buy into the 'health campaigns' that pretend to attack smoking by showing people dying of lung cancer, because I'll let you into another secret, one that many people involved in smoking cessation know full well:

These campaigns don't work. How many of these campaigns explain that there is no pleasure in smoking? None of them. How many explain that your subconscious mind mistakes the delayed reaction to nicotine for fear? None of them.

Instead, they always talk about the terrifying risks of smoking, risks that are already plastered on every cigarette advertisement and even on the packets themselves. These warnings do nothing more than frighten the hell out of every smoker who sees them, and what does fear make smokers do?

Smoke.

* * * * *

In fact, the cigarette industry and its vested interests would probably pay me a lot of money simply to shut up about the nicotine trick altogether and instead tell you about all the horrible diseases caused by smoking. But what's the point? If you're reading this book, the chances are that, at some point in your life you've already stumbled across the earth-shattering revelation *that smoking is bad for you.*

Do you ever feel like the world is going mad?

I do. Even now, I sometimes have to pinch myself in supermarkets when I see people queuing like nicotine-stained sheep, *actually queuing* towards brightly lit yellow banners that are screaming the words:

SMOKING CAUSES CANCER.

Members of the 'most advanced species' on this planet actually queuing to buy a product *with the threat of death directly advertised on the banners, the packets, the posters and everywhere else.* The scientists arrogantly declare that, somewhere in space there must be a species of life as advanced as us. What a laugh. What would we teach such a species? How to roll their own cigarettes? How to smoke in an aircraft toilet without getting caught?

Strange days.

* * * * *

Okay. I've now told you on several occasions that you won't be consciously making any decisions to stop smoking, and I mean it. However, this doesn't mean that these options don't physically exist. So, before I continue, it's only fair I should let you know that there are *two ways* to permanently get rid of the cravings to smoke – and only two.

The first way is to remove the fear response in your subconscious mind that causes it to tell you to smoke.

The second way is even simpler:

Die.

That's it. Those are your options.

Of course, you could argue that you've got a third choice (to simply keep smoking), but in fact this option is actually nothing more than a long-winded way of choosing the 'death' option. And don't bother looking for fake comfort in the statistics telling you that smoking only has a one in three chance of killing you. Statistics are the biggest (and oldest) form of deception on this planet.

> IF YOU SMOKE cigarettes, part of you is already dead – your freedom.

If you smoke cigarettes, *part of you is already dead – your freedom*. Your freedom to be calm, your freedom to taste food and drinks properly, your freedom to be fit, your freedom to sleep properly, your freedom to recover quickly from illnesses.

At this point, you may be excited, but you may also be in turmoil. Maybe you've spent so long kidding yourself that smoking must somehow be enjoyable that you're now struggling to accept that every cigarette you've ever smoked has been a total waste of time.

If so, close your eyes and look once again at the yellow supermarket banner you've seen a million times:

SMOKING CAUSES CANCER

… then consider this. Every time you've ever been under genuine threat, *your subconscious mind has always protected you*. Every time you've found yourself in a dangerous situation, your immediate reaction has been one of fear and self-preservation. And yet you smoke cigarettes, even though you know full well that smoking is the biggest cause of premature death on the planet. Well I've got news for you:

The only human emotion that can possibly override this level of fear is the fear of something even worse. Pleasure can't do it. Fear is what drives smoking.

About a hundred words into this book, I told you there is only one instinct stronger than the fear of death. It's the single worst fear a human being can endure: the fear of the unknown.

This fear sits at the centre of your affair with cigarettes like a black hole, sucking away your life and your confidence every single second of every single day. It drives your smoking, because the delayed sensation caused by smoking a cigarette gives you... fear without an obvious reason. Fake fear that then triggers real fear.

Each cigarette you've smoked has been the crucifix you've used to try to drive this ghost away, except it's never worked, has it? Every drag you've ever taken on a cigarette has simply kept this feeling going while providing the temporary illusion of 'relief'. You kept searching for this 'relief' again and again because there were two things you simply didn't know:

i) You didn't know that this sensation is simply a chemical imitation of fear, it was never the real thing, which means there was never any need for it to trigger *real* fear. ii) You didn't know that this sensation was caused by smoking, because it was a delayed response to nicotine and smoking always reduced the sensation slightly before causing it all over again.

Please let as many of your smoking friends as possible know this and even the ex-smokers you know who still crave cigarettes. Get on the phone to them, e-mail them with the address of the nicotine trick web site, write it on the back of a fag packet, but please, please tell them!

* * * * *

Let's take one final look at the misery of those millions of smokers who try to quit without making their subconscious minds know the facts – those who either use 'willpower' or simply 'hope for the best'.

What happens to them?

I'm afraid many of them go through absolute hell.

Take an example. When ex-smokers are at work and they see other smokers going for a cigarette break, they often feel irritable, anxious, insecure and physically tense. Why? Because their subconscious minds still believe that a cigarette will make them less stressed, so they think they're suffering because they're not smoking. *Their phobia kicks in more strongly than ever.*

Let's remind ourselves again why smoking is a total waste of time. Don't forget that *the delayed sensations caused by nicotine and fear respectively are not the same thing*, they just feel the same. This is why a cigarette cannot give pleasure or relaxation, all it can do is temporarily (and partially) reduce a physical sensation that your mind has confused with fear and anxiety, *a sensation that wouldn't even exist if you hadn't smoked the previous cigarette.*

Now let's make sure you're absolutely straight on what happens after you put a cigarette out.

About four days after you extinguish a cigarette (provided you don't smoke another one), the delayed feeling of tension caused by nicotine is gone, and so is any possibility of a cigarette reducing it. Period. *You can't reduce something that physically doesn't exist, temporarily or otherwise. It just isn't possible.*

ABOUT FOUR DAYS after you extinguish a cigarette (provided you don't smoke another one), the delayed feeling of tension caused by nicotine is gone, and so is any possibility of a cigarette reducing it. Period.

Let me show you how simple it really is. If you were driving and you were pulled over by the police, how scared would you be of failing a breathalyser test?

It depends, doesn't it? It depends on when you last had a drink.

Okay. Let's say you know for sure that you've not had a drink for five days. Now, how scared are you of failing this breathalyser test?

You're not scared, because *you physically cannot be over the limit. It's impossible.*

Does it make any difference if you appear nervous and stutter a bit while talking to the police officer? Well, it might make a difference to how he sees you, but will it make you any more or less likely to fail a breathalyser test?

No. It will make absolutely no difference at all.

So, predictably enough, you pass the breathalyser test. A few days later, you're unlucky enough to get stopped by the same officer. But you still haven't had a drink. So nothing's changed. Which means you're even less anxious than you were the previous time.

It's simple, right? A few days after you stop smoking, *you will no longer be experiencing the effects of tension caused by nicotine*. In the same way that you can't suddenly become drunk without having a drink, you can't get the delayed effects of nicotine without nicotine entering your body.

Sure, you can give yourself this sensation all over again by smoking a cigarette and then reducing it briefly with the one afterwards, but if you haven't actually got that sensation to start with, all you'll be doing is taking a ludicrously complicated route to feeling the same as you already do, which is not having the delayed reaction caused by nicotine! And it won't even work, *it will only reduce it slightly while causing it all over again!*

Why aren't you scared when it gets dark at night? Because you know it's going to be light in the morning. How do you know it's going to be light in the morning? Because it always has been in the past. Why won't you be scared of not smoking this time? Because your subconscious mind will know for sure that the delayed effects of nicotine are caused purely by smoking. It will also know that this feeling of tension can't hurt you. How will it know it can't hurt you? Because *it's never hurt you in the past*, the only thing which ever hurt you was what this sensation triggered:

Fear.

I read an internet article a few months ago which stated that the only 'pleasure' in smoking is the reduction in the withdrawal symptoms caused by the previous cigarette, and as cigarettes cause this feeling, there is no pleasure in smoking. The logic was absolutely correct. But what this internet article didn't fully explain is precisely *why* a feeling of physical tension can cause such problems in the first place. It described this feeling as a physical 'itch', which it isn't.

The article then went on to claim that craving a cigarette is a *conscious* decision, which is also wrong. The craving to smoke a cigarette is *one hundred per cent subconscious*.

Why? Because smoking is a fear response, and fear, like any other emotion, is only ever dealt with at a subconscious level. This fact is the missing link to the entire puzzle. When this sinks into your head, the picture becomes crystal clear.

Most people who have just 'stopped smoking' become anxious as soon as they even think about cigarettes, and they try to simply 'wish it away'. Some even go through the excruciating process of counting the days or even *hours* since they smoked their 'final' cigarette. In other words, they haven't given up at all, any more than someone who's holding their breath has decided to permanently give up breathing.

In addition, in the first couple of days, they've still got the feeling of tension caused by nicotine. By itself, this is no problem because smokers have this feeling all the time. But the problem is that *the fake anxiety and the real anxiety are now mixed together.* As a final insult, on top of all this is any other anxiety that exists simply as a result of everyday life.

In reality, even when a smoker is desperately struggling to stop, the total amount of physical tension directly caused by nicotine is small and it rapidly fades. But, because there's usually so much other stress associated with stopping smoking, what does the entire sensation feel like to most people in this situation?

It feels like the worst withdrawal symptoms in the world!

This is what smokers are really scared of when they think about quitting. Worse, they've heard horror stories from ex-smokers who are close to them, people they trust. As I said earlier, voodoo spells can kill people who believe in them. People can quite literally drop dead if the local witch doctor uses a spell on them.

How?

Fear.

The truth is, if you've ever gone more than a few days without a cigarette and then smoked, you were doing the equivalent of trying to remove a headache by taking an indigestion tablet. Any tension you had was no longer coming from nicotine, so smoking was never going to reduce it because *smoking can't reduce genuine stress, it can only reduce the fake version of it that is caused by the previous cigarette.*

You misunderstood what the feeling actually was. And, in the process, you gave yourself the delayed sensation of tension caused by nicotine all over again, without making even the slightest impression in any genuine feelings of stress.

It may all sound complicated, but it isn't really.

Throughout this book I've been circling you like a watchful bird, continually bringing your attention back to the central reason you smoke: the nicotine trick.

This is the problem with trying to stop smoking without knowing the facts. If you quit and then start worrying about cravings and smoking, you obviously suffer stress, and this feels like 'withdrawal symptoms', which makes you want to smoke. *You actually summon the demon simply by thinking about it.*

> THE TRUTH IS, if you've ever gone more than a few days without a cigarette and then smoked, you were doing the equivalent of trying to remove a headache by taking an indigestion tablet.

This is why you can't stop smoking and then hope the cravings miraculously go away by themselves. It might seem to work for a few days or weeks, but the connections are still in your head, like a time-bomb waiting to go off.

* * * * *

There are days when I totally despair of the way smokers think, but then I remind myself of how warped my own thinking was before I discovered the information I've put down in this book (and on the web site, in the workshops, on the CDs and so on).

Every single year, tens of millions of people split up with their cigarettes, only to go crawling back to them. Why? Because it ended badly. Their subconscious minds were still clinging to an illusion. *They were still frightened.*

Okay. We're almost there. You've almost beaten the nicotine trick. You've listened as I've carefully explained the truth behind your affair with cigarettes.

Your patience is about to pay off.

Anti-climax

Congratulations. You are now in an incredible position of strength. Let me explain precisely why.

Simply knowing that smoking is a phobia is priceless, because this knowledge by itself permanently destroys any illusion that smoking is pleasurable. In fact, some smokers I've known who didn't want to stop smoking in the slightest have expressed their extreme annoyance after I've explained the nicotine trick to them. They complained that,

'Cigarettes don't feel the same any more.'

And even,

'Couldn't you have kept it to yourself?'

Strangely, I can feel some sympathy with these people, although I must point out that I didn't personally create the chemical properties of nicotine; these properties exist by sheer chemical chance.

Anyway, you finally know how smoking works, or more accurately, *why it doesn't*.

What now?

Now we come to the exciting bit. Transferring what your conscious mind now knows directly into your subconscious mind, destroying the phobia that drives your smoking. Some people are worried at this point, because they assume I want to hypnotise them, and they've heard the

SIMPLY KNOWING THAT smoking is a phobia is priceless, because this knowledge by itself permanently destroys any illusion that smoking is pleasurable.

horror stories of people being humiliated and demeaned by stage hypnotists. But *it didn't take a hypnotist to make you start smoking*, so there is absolutely no need for you to be hypnotised by one in order to stop.

This doesn't mean that we're not going to get

into your subconscious mind, but we are going to take a slightly different route to that of hypnotism.

How?

Well, I can't tell you *when* to stop smoking, because this choice is going to be made by your subconscious mind.

But from this point onwards, you're only going to smoke by going through a simple, three-step process that will enable your subconscious mind to finally see what's really happening. This will cause it to let go of the fear response that drives smoking.

> FROM THIS POINT onwards, you're only going to smoke by going through a simple, three-step process that will enable your subconscious mind to finally see what's really happening.

Based on my experience, sometimes this happens almost immediately, but usually it takes a few days. The important thing isn't that it happens instantly, but *permanently*.

Okay. Before continuing, I want you to make sure you're ready to smoke a cigarette, and that you have about ten minutes during which you're unlikely to be disturbed or interrupted.

Please don't light the cigarette until I ask you

to. Now, here's what we're going to do. First, we're going to use a *visualisation technique based on the snake analogy I mentioned earlier*, a technique that will create a subtle change in your subconscious mind. It's a technique similar to that used by psychologists dealing with other phobias and it's based on a simple principle:

Your conscious mind finds it easier to absorb ideas that are presented using words, numbers and logic. This is how this book has explained the nicotine trick to you. But your subconscious mind absorbs ideas much better when they're presented in a way that is *sensory* and, in particular, *visual*.

STEP 1 – SNAKE VISUALISATION

Let me describe what you're going to visualise. Then I'll explain how to make it really powerful. By doing this, you'll be creating *a new perception of nicotine* in your subconscious mind, one that your mind will start to use each time you smoke.

I want you to imagine being bitten by a snake and injected with mild, non-lethal venom (nicotine). The venom won't cause physical pain, but your body will immediately start reacting to it, which will trigger a gradually building sensation of painless physical tension. It will then take about four days for your body to get rid of the venom, during which time the feeling of tension will slowly fade away to nothing.

Now, each time you get bitten by this snake, the process will start all over again, beginning with a mild feeling of tension. What this means is that, once this feeling has grown to full strength, *getting bitten again will appear to reduce it.*

In fact it won't do any such thing. Far from *reducing* it, it will simply *delay your recovery* by starting it from scratch all over again. In other words, if you're ever going to be rid of this feeling, you need to *let the poison simply run its course*, rather than repeatedly allowing yourself to be bitten again, which just keeps causing it to start from scratch. Fortunately, letting the poison run its course in this way no longer frightens you in the slightest.

Why not?

Because you now know exactly how this venom works, which means you know exactly what to expect. Nothing more than a feeling of painless physical tension that will fade away after about four days. In fact, *even after two days* it will have faded to the same level that you feel immediately after you get bitten by the snake. The difference is that this time it will continue to fade, rather than rising all over again.

There's no fear, no confusion. Just a simple choice. Either allow the snake to keep biting you and keep restarting the feeling of tension at a lower level, or let the poison run its course and be rid of this feeling altogether.

Even better, as soon as the feeling of tension starts to fade, nothing in the entire universe can make it start again unless you get bitten again. And even this is under your control because the snake needs your permission to bite you.

In other words, the only way to keep experiencing this feeling of tension is to keep deliberately getting bitten. Also understand that *there is no reason on earth for your body's natural reaction to the venom to frighten you*. In fact, it would be far more frightening if your body *didn't react* to being bitten, because it would mean it didn't know how to cope with the venom.

The next step, when I ask you, is to go through this simple visualisation once more, but with your eyes *closed*. And this time, I want you to start adding your own detail to it. Attach the exact feeling you understand as 'nicotine withdrawal symptoms' to your body's reaction to being bitten by the snake. A delayed feeling of mild, painless tension in your face, shoulders, chest and stomach. Understand that you've allowed this snake to bite you thousands of times, and your body has started to recover every time, which means the venom isn't fatal in small doses – all it does it makes you feel tense. And, if you avoid being bitten by the snake, nothing can stop your body from finally being calm again, just as it was before you suffered the first of all those snake bites.

> DON'T FEEL EMBARRASSED about adding bizarre or colourful details. It won't make it less real, it will make it more real.

Don't feel embarrassed about adding bizarre or colourful details. It won't make it less real, *it will make it more real.*

Last week I took a phone call from a workshop attendee (a very impatient type) who'd been struggling for a day or so to imagine the snake visualisation convincingly and who had suddenly, quite literally, *dreamed it in his sleep* in an amazing level of detail. For years he'd smoked

Benson & Hedges, and in his dream the snake was a large gold cobra, with the intricate B&H logo along its body. But it wasn't a nightmare, because the snake no longer represented a threat to him.

Having identified the snake with the brand he'd smoked, the rest of the visualisation sank effortlessly into his subconscious mind, his phobia disappeared, and with it his desire to smoke.

Don't forget that this snake is different from every other snake because it *needs your permission* to bite you, and even if it does bite you the venom will only cause physical tension, not pain. So enjoy adding your own detail to the experience. Experiment with it. *Make it feel like a real memory*. Take as long as you need. Don't worry if it seems a strange thing to do. You use your imagination like this all the time without even realising it.

Do it now.

You've just created a completely new 'memory' inside your brain. It may not mean much to you

DON'T FORGET THAT this snake is different from every other snake because it needs your permission to bite you, and even if it does bite you the venom will only cause physical tension, not pain.

just yet, but your subconscious mind now has a new way of 'feeling' nicotine, one that, although imagined, has been chosen because it reflects reality, *which is why it works so well.*

It doesn't make any difference that you imagined it. *Nothing can now stop your subconscious mind from using this memory whenever it wants to.*

From this point onwards, you'll now notice that this snake visualisation seems to enter your mind at random times for 'no reason at all'. You may even find yourself dreaming about it. In fact, there will be a very good reason it keeps coming into your head, as you'll see.

STEP 2 – DIAPHRAGMATIC BREATH

Okay. You're going to smoke a cigarette in a few moments. But, before you do, there's another step you need to take. Right now, I want you to *slowly take a massive deep breath, raising your stomach as much as possible as you breathe in.* Completely fill your lungs. Hold it for a few moments, then let it out slowly and completely. This is called *diaphragmatic breathing.*

And again. Take another massive, deep breath, slowly release it, and then carry on breathing in your normal way.

Your brain has just released hormones called *endorphins* into your bloodstream – natural tranquilising chemicals that will very quickly make you feel a sensation of increased relaxation spreading through your body, starting with your face and chest. There's a good reason for doing this, an important fact I've saved until now.

When you light a cigarette, *the first thing you instinctively do is take a deep breath of smoke and hold it in your lungs for a few seconds, in order to get as much nicotine as possible.*

Usually, you then smoke the rest of the cigarette by taking much shallower breaths.

Without you knowing it, this deep breath also releases the same endorphins that your diaphragmatic breathing just did a few moments ago, *which slightly reduces the agitating effects of the smoke.*

But here's the trick. By deliberately causing these endorphins to be released *before* smoking the cigarette, you ensure that *your subconscious brain doesn't get the same effect all over again when you take your first drag on the cigarette.* This means that any illusion of relaxation will be diluted even further, and your subconscious mind will become even less frightened of letting go of smoking.

Let's prove it.

STEP 3 – ALLOW YOURSELF TO BE BITTEN (BY SMOKING A CIGARETTE)

Okay. It's time to let yourself get bitten. Don't forget that you've done this many times, and it's never done anything other than 'reset' the feeling of nicotine-induced tension back to the start and cause it to start growing again.

Now, I want you to light the cigarette and start smoking it but, as you take the first drag, *imagine the snake biting you, injecting you with venom which will eventually make you feel stressed and tense. Remind yourself that if you've already got this venom inside you, being bitten will 'reset' the feeling of tension back to the beginning.* You don't need to make any effort to think about the rest of the visualisation, because your subconscious mind will now fill in the blanks for you automatically. Just concentrate as I explain what is now physically happening.

Almost immediately, you will feel a physical sensation of dizziness and numbness, caused mainly by carbon monoxide. You may feel a slight tingling in your fingers and toes. People who gas themselves with car exhausts feel a similar sensation just before they pass out. Fortunately, you've not taken in enough to kill you, just enough to make you feel slightly dazed and light-headed. In your mouth you will taste a vague sweetness. This is caused by additives such as *sugar and cocoa*, which are added to the paper in order to make the pollutants in the smoke less irritating to the inside of your lungs and mouth.

> YOU DON'T NEED to make any effort to think about the rest of the visualisation, because your subconscious mind will now fill in the blanks for you automatically.

About fifteen seconds after your first drag, the nicotine in the smoke has already flooded the nicotine receptor cells in your brain. This means you have now created a delayed chemical reaction that will cause a gradual build-up of physical tension in your body. (If you weren't to smoke again, this sensation would disappear in about four days.)

Now concentrate as I explain exactly what else is happening as you continue to smoke. Your heart is beating faster and your blood pressure has increased, because you've got more adrenalin in your bloodstream. Your central nervous system is churning with poisonous chemicals, just like it was the first time you ever smoked.

You may think that this cigarette doesn't feel any different from any other cigarettes you've smoked, and you're right. *It doesn't feel physically different, because it isn't physically different.* But what *is* different is the way in which your subconscious mind will now respond to what happens inside your body after you've finished smoking this cigarette, the way it will now see the build-up of tension as being directly caused by the cigarette you're smoking right now, the way *it will stop being scared when it notices it.* You'll know what I mean when it happens.

Please smoke the rest of the cigarette, even if you don't feel like it. Don't carry on reading past the end of this sentence until you've put it out.

WHAT HAPPENS NEXT

Let me explain what happens now.

Some smokers go through this three-step process just once or twice and lose their phobia completely, along with any future cravings to smoke. But most people need to repeat it for a few days before the desire to smoke disappears altogether. Think of it this way. When you were learning to ride a bike, you may have fallen off more times than your best friend did, but what difference did it make? *In the end, it just clicked, and when it did, that was it.* It may be many years since you last rode a bike, but do you really doubt that you could do it if you had to?

> WHEN YOU WERE learning to ride a bike, you may have fallen off more times than your best friend did, but what difference did it make? In the end, it just clicked, and when it did, that was it.

Without you even trying, your subconscious mind will now start carefully processing the new information you've just given it. As a result, you'll start to notice that, at the times you usually get a desire to smoke, there's now a vague 'feeling' in the back of your mind, which is seeing a different view of what smoking would actually do. But, until you have absolutely no desire to smoke, I want you to override this feeling and *actually force the reality of smoking on to your subconscious mind by using the three-step process you've just used.*

Your subconscious mind won't like this at all, and it will rapidly become even more annoyed and irritated by the thought of smoking. As a result, you'll soon realise that, by the time you get to step three, the thought of a cigarette is becoming increasingly alien to you. When this happens, smoke it anyway. Always complete the process whenever you start it.

All you need to do now is to promise yourself that any further cigarettes you smoke will be smoked using this three-step process. That's the only commitment you need to make. You're going to leave the final decision of when to stop smoking to your subconscious mind, but by following these steps, you ensure that it will let go of the phobia as soon as possible.

> ALL YOU NEED to do now is to promise yourself that any further cigarettes you smoke will be smoked using this three-step process. That's the only commitment you need to make.

Let's remind ourselves once again what the three steps are:

- **Step 1 – snake visualisation**

- **Step 2 – two diaphragmatic breaths**

- **Step 3 – allow yourself to be bitten (by smoking a cigarette)**

If necessary, write these three steps down on a card or a piece of paper and carry them with you. Maybe you'll want to write a few notes for the snake visualisation, a few cues to trigger the experience as vividly as possible.

Also, from now *until you're absolutely sure you've lost the desire to smoke, let the snake visualisation drift into your mind whenever you're relaxing, or just before you go to sleep when you're drowsy.* Do it slowly, lingering on each detail. Don't ever forget that this visualisation represents the

> JUST REMEMBER THIS. At no point in your life has your body ever wanted you to smoke.

simple truth of smoking, so really make it part of you, *allow yourself to 'feel it'*, get comfortable with it.

Just remember this. At no point in your life has your body ever wanted you to smoke. Only your subconscious mind is even capable of telling you to smoke, and it will only do this if it becomes frightened. Have confidence in its ability to protect you. Even as you read this sentence, it is already absorbing the 'new' reality of the cigarette you just smoked. Of course, it may continue to test this reality for a little while with urges to smoke. If so, *don't fight these urges or feel discouraged that they've happened.* Your subconscious mind will let go when it's ready, believe me.

You'll know that this has happened when you can 'feel' that smoking a cigarette would do *nothing more than make you feel tense.* This may already have happened as a result of going through this three-step process just once, but most probably it will take a few days before you feel like this whenever the thought of smoking occurs to you. Until this happens, the three-step process will make sure that each time you smoke, your subconscious mind is allowed to see the reality of smoking that has been hidden from it for so long.

Afterword

I've tried to keep this book concise and focused. That way, you can now read it again in just a couple of hours if you need to, to make sure you understand exactly how the nicotine trick works, to make sure you 'get it' completely.

One very important point. Be aware that, even when your subconscious mind has let go of smoking, you'll still encounter situations that remind you of cigarettes. So do I. Don't worry about it. These are not cravings. They're simply memories. *When those memories were made, you didn't know about the nicotine trick. Your subconscious mind will now process these memories in the light of what it now knows.*

You don't need to avoid going to pubs or restaurants, nor do you need to avoid smokers. You won't lose your friends, or miss out on any good times. You're now in the process of stepping out of a phobia based on lies and confusion into clear sunshine that is *nothing less than the simple truth.*

BE AWARE THAT, even when your subconscious mind has let go of smoking, you'll still encounter situations which remind you of cigarettes. So do I.

If you wish to give me your feedback or experiences, or you want an update on the very latest technology being used to deliver the nicotine trick, look at the nicotine trick web site for details (www.nicotinetrick.com.) By the time you read this, there will also be a recorded information line for you to call.

The next time you're stressed by anything, *try taking those two slow, deep breaths – or three or four in an emergency – using your stomach.* The endorphins subsequently released into your bloodstream will relax you in less than thirty seconds. Remember: this is the only part of smoking a cigarette that has ever 'worked', and you've still got it. So you haven't lost anything, *and you've gained everything.*

Finally, remember that when you no longer have any desire to smoke, many smokers you know will now be extremely jealous and embarrassed, even if they refuse to admit it. If they express this embarrassment by trying to tempt you to smoke, I want you to realise that they're not doing it to hurt you, they're doing it because *what you've achieved has made them feel even more frightened and insecure than they already were.*

* * * * *

It seems strange to bring this book to such an abrupt end, but that really is just about it. You now know as much as I do about the nicotine trick. We've been on a fascinating journey together, one that taken us to some weird and wonderful places. I hope you've enjoyed reading this book as much as I've enjoyed writing it. I won't wish you luck from this point onwards, for a very important reason…

… you no longer need it.